CASEBOOK FOR MANAGEMENT INFORMATION SYSTEMS

Eighth Edition

George P. Schell
Raymond McLeod, Jr.

Upper Saddle River, New Jersey 07458

Acquisitions editor: Bob Horan
Assistant editor: Lori Cerreto
Production editor: Carol Zaino
Manufacturer: Technical Communication Services

Copyright ©2001 by Prentice-Hall, Inc., Upper Saddle River, New Jersey, 07458. All rights reserved. Printed in the United States of America. This publication is protected by copyright, and permission should be obtained from the publisher prior to any prohibited reproduction, storage in a retrieval system, or transmission in any form or by any means, electronic, mechanical, photocopying, recording, or likewise. For information regarding permission(s), write to: Rights and Permissions Department.

ISBN 0-13-061043-7

10 9 8 7 6 5 4 3 2

CONTENTS

Preface vii
Chapter 1 - Solution of a Case Problem 1
Chapter 2 - Documentation of a Case Problem Solution 9
Chapter 3 - A Sample Case Problem 15
Chapter 4 - Solution of the Sample Problem 18
Chapter 5 - A Sample Solution 27

CASES

Council of 100 32
University Computing 45
Ecologix Technologies 59
Midwest Farm Supplies 71
Campus Bookstore 84
Canadian Data Systems, Ltd. 97
Baltimore Door & Window 114

To Shar and Glenn
RMcL

To the managers who let us learn from their mistakes.
GPS

PREFACE

The ability to view an organization as a system, to gather information in a systematic fashion, and to communicate both orally and in writing are important business skills. In today's world of electronic communications, these skills are more important than ever and they will be even more important in the future. Using the case study method is the best way to develop these skills while in college. A business problem can be brought into the classroom in written form, and you can assume the responsibilities of a manager in solving that problem. Your findings can be presented in writing to your instructor, or presented orally to your instructor and your classmates, or both.

Our interest in the case study method and our approach to solution began while we were undergraduate and graduate students. Later, we applied the methods in industry as systems analysts and consultants. While the names of the companies and the people in the cases in this book are fictitious, most of the situations are based on our experiences.

We are strong believers in the use of the systems approach in solving business problems and recommend it for solving case problems as well. The systems approach is explained and illustrated in the first five chapters of this *Casebook*. This book is unique in that it not only contains case problems to solve, but it also provides you with the methodology to use in solving them.

Although the cases are designed with the systems approach in mind, the book has a built-in flexibility in that you have alternative ways of presenting your problem solutions. You can use the format of a written report explained in Chapter 2, you can answer the questions that appear at the end of each case, or your instructor can specify some other format. Your instructor will tell you which approach to take.

The 8th Edition of the *Casebook* has the same case names and general themes as the cases in the 6th Edition. However, the cases have been revised to reflect the content of the 8th Edition of *Management Information Systems* by McLeod and Schell. The same case names and themes are used to allow instructors the opportunity to migrate from one edition to the other with minimal disruption of class materials.

This 8th Edition of the *Casebook* could not be written except with the understanding of managers and businesses that the authors have worked with over the years. It is not easy to admit a mistake, much less let the mistake be published so that the whole world can find out. But the managers and businesses that provide the basis for these cases have understood that students need a forum for trying out their skills of analysis before they enter the business world. Take heed of their problems and do not forget that what might seem to be an easy problem when presented in a classroom can be overwhelming and difficult when presented under the time constraints and pressure of the manager's work load.

Raymond McLeod, Jr.
Austin, Texas

George P. Schell
Wilmington, North Carolina

CHAPTER 1
SOLUTION OF A CASE PROBLEM

This chapter describes the systems approach in a summary fashion and relates the approach to classroom situations. A fuller explanation is provided in Chapter 6 of *Management Information Systems*, 8th Edition, by McLeod and Schell. The classroom orientation should not imply that the systems approach has no value in the real world of business. Nothing could be farther from the truth. The primary objective of the case study method is to develop a real world problem-solving ability.

You will probably become involved in case studies in other courses. You should be able to use the systems approach described here equally well in the other classes, whether they be in business policy, personnel management, marketing, or the like. However, the approach that you are expected to follow in another course might not be the systems approach. This does not mean that the other method is right and this is wrong, or vice versa. It simply means that each instructor usually has a preferred technique for problem solving, and wants you to learn how to use it. In those cases where you are given latitude in selecting a problem-solving technique, the systems approach is recommended for consideration. After use by the authors in different types of courses over a period of years, there has been no case situation that required a different approach.

Most instructors recognize the limitations of an approach that is a rigid set of steps to be followed in all situations. Such an approach is referred to as a "cook book" approach, implying that the user does not really have to understand what is being done but only follow a series of instructions. The systems approach is not a cook book approach. Even though the systems approach involves a series of steps, the steps represent a general outline that must be adapted to the particular problem situation. Applying the systems approach effectively requires insight, analysis, and innovation.

The systems approach is not a quick and easy method. The technique requires practice--most of us never reach the point where we feel that we have completely mastered it. You can expect to spend your entire business career sharpening your problem-solving skills.

THE CASE SOLUTION PROCESS

You usually have a number of days to solve a case problem from the time it is assigned until the solution is due. The solution may have to be expressed in the form of a written report, an oral report, or both. Regardless of the report medium, the format is rarely the same as the sequence that you follow in solving the problem.

Most report formats consist of three main elements (in order):

1. Problem definition
2. Problem solution
3. Support for the solution

These reports are much like newspaper articles; the headlines and the first few paragraphs give the important facts with the supporting data included toward the end.

When you follow the process of solving the problem, the three main elements (in order) are:

1. Problem definition
2. Problem analysis
3. Problem solution

First you define the problem to be solved. Then you analyze the situation so that you understand it. Finally you devise a solution. You must recognize this difference in sequence between the report format and the solution process in order to understand the descriptions in these first five chapters.

Defining the Problem

In taking the systems approach, the manager first defines the problem. The same is true for the student in case situations. You can assume that there is a problem to be solved. If not, the case would not be presented.

Problems Can Be Both Good and Bad

It is natural to think of problems as being bad, and most of the time this is true. It is especially true of written case problems that students are expected to solve. Invariably, the cases deal with something that has gone wrong or is about to go wrong in a firm.

Although you may encounter fewer cases where the problem is something that is going better than expected, you should be aware that such a possibility exists. When actual performance exceeds expectations, management reacts to take advantage of the opportunity and achieve the same superior performance in other areas.

You Do Not Have to Know Everything

In a real business situation, the manager usually has a good understanding of the problem area. The manager is familiar with the firm, its history, its goals and objectives, its policies and procedures, its facilities and equipment, its people, and its organizational structure.

Sometimes all of this knowledge can actually muddy the water by complicating the situation with a multitude of facts, a situation called "information overload." This is one reason why managers often call in such outside experts as management consultants to help solve problems. The outsider can focus directly on the problem area without being distracted by what is irrelevant.

Think of Yourself as a Consultant

The consultant role is a good one for you to play as you solve a case problem. Assume that the firm's chief executive, such as the president, has reason to believe that a problem exists or might exist in the future, and has asked you to help solve it.

Some case situations present relatively minor or modest problems. When the general situation is quite good, your attention should be focused on the finer points. Do not be afraid to be especially critical. This is the only way to ensure that the problem you are expected to solve does not go undetected. As you search for problems, leave no stone unturned.

Read the Case More Than One Time

Just as the consultant first has to gain an overall view of the situation, you also must become familiar with the facts. This familiarity is gained by reading and studying the case. It will probably be necessary to read the case more than one time. Some cases are rather lengthy and contain too many facts to handle in one pass through the narrative.

Give Yourself Enough Time

Your first reading will only acquaint you with the problem situation. Your initial reaction may very well be "There are really a lot of facts here." Your task, then, is to separate the relevant from the irrelevant, and that takes time.

Allow yourself at least one full day from the time you first read the case until you begin a serious analysis. During this time, think about the case as you take a shower or walk across the campus. Consider alternative problems and solutions. Ask yourself "If I could do only one thing, would that take care of most of the problems that the firm faces?" This time for thinking through the case is the key to the solution process. Do not cut it short.

The Hierarchy of Problem Areas

The application of the systems approach to the solution of business problems recognizes a hierarchy of systems levels. Figure 1.1 illustrates this concept. The firm is a system that exists in a larger environmental supersystem and consists of subsystems.

The systems approach requires that you inspect each of the levels in sequence from the supersystem to the system to the subsystems. Very often, you will identify problems on more than one level. In such a case, the hierarchy does not necessarily determine the relative importance of the problems. A problem on a lower level may be of major importance while one on a higher level may be less critical. As a general rule, however, lower-level problems cannot be completely solved until <u>related</u> problems on higher levels have been corrected.

Environment (the Supersystem)

Financial Community	Stockholders	Local Community	Customers
Labor	Competition	Suppliers	Government

The System

The Firm

Subsystems of the Firm

Marketing	Manufacturing	Finance

Figure 1.1

System Levels

Location of Problems in the System

When a particular system level of the firm is being studied, each part of the system should be analyzed. This analysis should proceed in the following sequence:

1. The *objectives and/or standards* that establish the desired level of the system's performance
2. The *outputs*, such as finished goods or services, that the system produces for its environment
3. The *management* and the organizational structure
4. The *information processor*, such as a computer, that transforms data into information for management
5. The *inputs*, such as raw materials, that flow into the system from its environment, and the *input resources*, such as receiving and quality control inspection areas, that process the inputs
6. The *processes* that transform the inputs into outputs
7. The *output resources*, such as shipping docks and truck fleets, that distribute the output to the environment

Figure 1.2 shows this sequence. The lower portion of the diagram represents the flow of physical resources through the firm and the upper portion is concerned with the management of the physical flow. The dotted lines show how data is gathered from the physical system and entered into the information processor. The solid lines represent information and physical flows in the physical system. The information processor transforms the data into information that is presented to management. Management compares the information with the objectives and/or standards and makes decisions that keep the physical system on course. By making the quantitative performance standards available to the information processor, it can relieve management of determining whether the system is performing as it should. The way that the information processor calls the manager's attention to selected activity enables the manager to practice management by exception.

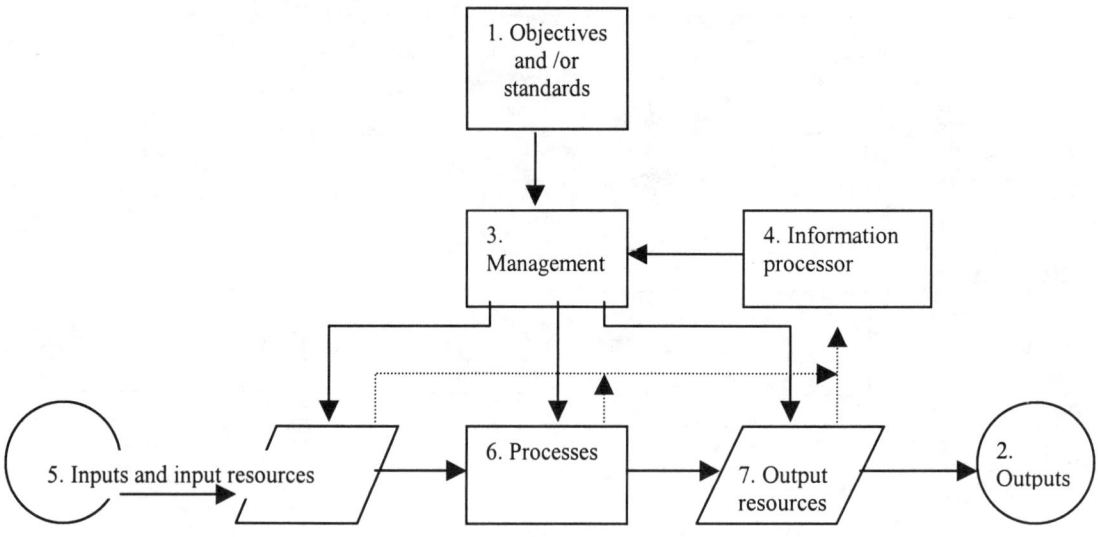

Figure 1.2

System Parts Are Analyzed in Sequence

Use of Case Solution Forms

It is a good idea to take notes of the important points as you read the case. The blank forms contained in this *Casebook* are intended to be used in this manner. The forms help you learn the systems approach by organizing your notes. As you become a more experienced problem solver the forms will become less necessary, but you will always have to gather the needed information and assemble it in a usable format.

Some of the entries that you make on the forms may appear to be important during your initial reading, but may later turn out to have no relationship to the problem. This is simply the process of refining a large amount of data into a usable quantity of information.

Hints in Defining the Problem

Unfortunately, there is no general formula to follow in problem definition. The process depends on the particular case situation but some valuable clues can be used to narrow the choice to a more specific area.

The course of study provides the most basic clue. While this might seem obvious, there are usually a wide variety of approaches that can be taken to solution but the one that the instructor undoubtedly will prefer is one that ties in with the course. An example is a case problem involving a large metropolitan police department. If the case is being used in a sociology or urban studies class, the students might recognize the problem as the difficulty of law enforcement in a large, complex social system. In a management information class, however, the students might be expected to recognize the lack of objectives in the police department and the impact this is having on the information system. Both courses could use the same case to address completely different problems.

Another clue often can be obtained by relating the case to course material that has just been covered. If the case is assigned after you have completed a study of planning, there is a good chance that the case provides an example of how some of that planning material can be applied. Be careful when applying this clue, however, since instructors have been known to assign cases out of sequence.

In addition to the use of clues provided by the course and text, there is also the possibility that you can obtain help in problem definition from classmates, other students, instructors, or people in business. Your instructor may not want you to discuss the assignments with your classmates but may be more receptive to you seeking help from people outside the class. Quite often businesspersons have faced the same or similar problems and can provide valuable insights. Ask your instructor to define the extent to which you can solicit problem definition help from others.

In addition to these human resources, you are always encouraged to conduct literature research in the problem area. Books, professional journals, popular magazines, government publications, and even newspapers can often provide helpful information. The library is a powerful resource in problem definition and solution, and, as a college student, you know how to use that resource. Take advantage of your library research skills.

Problems and Not Symptoms

The cardinal rule in this analytic process is to be certain that what you identify as a problem is really a problem and not just a symptom of a problem. For example, a person suffers from recurring headaches and decides to go to the doctor for help. The doctor examines the person and determines that the headaches are being caused by nervous tension. The headaches are a symptom and the tension is the problem. Similar examples can be found in business where the manager's attention is attracted to a particular situation because of a symptom (such as a drop in profits), and then he or she probes to find the root cause. The <u>root cause</u> is the condition or conditions that you will attempt to change in the case of a bad problem, or capitalize on in the case of a good problem.

In fact, a better term than "problem" is "cause of the trouble" or "cause of the opportunity." What you really want to know is the basic cause of certain events or conditions that may be especially harmful or beneficial to the firm.

To get to the root cause, it might be necessary for you to follow a <u>symptom chain</u>--a series of symptoms, one leading to another. For example, assume that management of a printing company becomes alarmed about the number of refunds being given to customers. The customers are dissatisfied with their purchases and ask for their money back. The initial symptom is the excessive refund amount. This condition leads first to the financial accounting system that issues the refunds. If this system checks out OK, the attention can be directed at the production system that does the printing. Study of this area may reveal that the cause of the excessive refunds is poor quality. The poor quality may be caused by low morale of production workers, which, in turn, is caused by poor fringe benefits. In this scenario, a symptom chain (excessive refunds, poor quality, and low morale) leads to the root cause (poor fringe benefits). Management solves the problem by addressing the fringe benefits issue.

The problem solver follows the chain of symptoms, asking for each "What is causing this?" When the cause is some basic action or inaction that is not stimulated by some other, more basic, action or inaction, then the root cause of the problem has been identified. As you gain experience, you will become more skilled at knowing when you reach the problem that you want to solve.

As a general rule, you solve the problem that you are qualified to solve. Perhaps the real root cause is the fact that the president's mother made her or him eat broccoli as a child. However, at this point in time you are not equipped to address that problem. If you are a systems analyst, you most often address problems relating to the system's objectives and/or standards, management, and information processor. If you are an industrial engineer, you are especially adept at solutions in the physical system of the firm.

This identification of the root cause is the most important and the most difficult step in the problem solving process. In developing this skill, experience is the best teacher.

Most Roads Lead to the Manager

Since everything that occurs within a firm is due to some action or inaction by personnel, a problem can eventually be traced to a person or persons. Since management is responsible for everything that happens in the firm, everything can eventually be traced to management.

For this reason, the management element in the system structure will almost always be related to one of the other elements. If a problem exists with objectives and/or standards, it is because management has not properly established them. The same can be said for organization, the information system, and the physical system.

This point is significant. <u>Whatever the problem in a firm, management invariably is involved</u>. Your task is to find the management position or level with responsibility for the problem area and to aim your recommendations at that manager or group of managers.

In seeking the level where responsibility for the problem lies, all roads do not lead to the president. Although this person is technically responsible for everything that happens in the firm, lower-level managers are responsible for their own areas.

Too Many Problems?

The best situation is to have only a single problem to solve. Then, the solution can be straightforward. However, your instructor may want to see evidence that you have recognized <u>all</u> of the problems. One way to accomplish this is to list all of the problems and then select one for solution. You can eliminate the other problems from consideration by stating that they are outside the scope of your study. Your instructor should advise you how she or he feels about this strategy.

A good technique in limiting your task to a single problem is to address only one of the numbered elements in the Figure 1.2 diagram. Determine the defective element with the highest priority, using the sequence numbers, and solve that particular problem. For example, if the firm has defective management, objectives, and information processor, address the problem of defective objectives since it is the system element with the highest priority. Of course, if defects in management are hindering the establishment of objectives, those defects will have to be overcome during the process of establishing the objectives.

EVALUATING THE SOLUTIONS

Most business problems can be solved in a number of ways. Just as a manager must identify a number of feasible alternatives, you are expected to go through the same analytical process.

You must recognize that all of the alternatives, including the one recommended, will possess both advantages and disadvantages. The advantage of one alternative often will be a disadvantage of another. For example, an advantage of outsourcing the development of a complex system is that the outsourcer is likely to be experienced in such a project. This advantage corresponds to a disadvantage of developing the system in-house where such experience does not exist. By the same token, the advantage of self sufficiency of the in-house approach corresponds to the disadvantage of dependency on an outside organization that goes with the outsourcing.

In identifying the advantages and disadvantages of each alternative, you must not assume more than the data in the case permits. The items identified as advantages or disadvantages must be supportable by information in the case or by information gained as a result of additional research. For example, if the case includes no specifications of computing equipment currently being used, then no concrete statements can be made about potential cost savings or performance improvements that can be achieved through the use of other types of equipment.

Choice of Alternatives

The alternatives depend on the case; however, some guidelines can be followed to assure that a good set is selected. First of all, the alternatives rarely represent the choice of either doing something or not doing something. You can assume that the case demands something to be done. This eliminates the alternative of "Leave the system as it is." When a firm has a problem, inaction is not an alternative.

The alternatives should also represent several different methods of achieving the same solution. They should not represent different solutions that could be used together or in some combination. For example, if the problem is lack of education at the middle-management level in setting performance standards, the alternatives would consider various means by which an education program might be achieved--meetings, formal courses, industry seminars, and so on.

An example of different solutions used together would be the consideration of reorganization, standards setting, management education, and implementation of an information system. These possibilities do not represent different methods of achieving a single solution, but, instead, separate solutions. In fact, these are solutions to separate problems. Each can be further evaluated in terms of alternative solutions. Different methods of reorganization can be considered, as well as different approaches to standards setting, education, and information system design. The initial identification of these avenues as alternatives represents problem-solving on too high a level. The problem should be further subdivided to permit more effective solution.

Figure 1.3 illustrates this example. Each problem area (organization, objectives and/or standards, management education, and realtime information system) should be addressed to determine which one, or ones, should be pursued for solution. Once selected, the different alternatives for each problem area should be identified and evaluated in terms of advantages and disadvantages.

ACHIEVING THE SOLUTION

Once the best alternative has been selected, you have the responsibility to present a program that can be followed to implement the solution. As an example, if the problem is the lack of a responsive information network and the solution is to implement a computerized system, you should explain how the firm should go about putting the computerized system into operation. Obviously, such a plan can only be presented within the scope of the required report and can employ only material pertinent to the case. You are not expected to formulate the same type of detailed implementation plan that would be required in a company.

This responsibility to recommend an implementation plan forces you to consider only alternatives that are feasible for the organization being studied. Take the situation, for example, where a president is deficient in some way. Perhaps he or she cannot delegate responsibility. Whereas the alternative "Replace the president" might solve the problem, it might not be feasible. For one thing, the president might own the company. But, even on lower organizational levels, replacing someone is usually the last resort. Rather than replacement, the preferred approach is to change the personnel weaknesses into strengths.

Solutions that are not feasible become apparent when you try to describe the implementation.

PRESENTING THE SOLUTION

At this point, you have familiarized yourself with the case, identified and defined the problems, considered alternative solutions, selected the best alternative, and prepared a plan to guide the implementation of the solution. The remaining task is to present the solution to the person or persons who will authorize its implementation. A format that you can follow for a written report is included in the next chapter.

Problems: Not Alternatives

Organization	Objectives and/or Standards	Management Education	Realtime Information System

- alternative 1
  -- advantages
  -- disadvantages
	- alternative 1
	  -- advantages
	  -- disadvantages
		- alternative 1
		  -- advantages
		  -- disadvantages
			- alternative 1
			  -- advantages
			  -- disadvantages

- alternative 2
  -- advantages
  -- disadvantages
	- alternative 2
	  -- advantages
	  -- disadvantages
		- alternative 2
		  -- advantages
		  -- disadvantages
			- alternative 2
			  -- advantages
			  -- disadvantages

- alternative n
  -- advantages
  -- disadvantages
	- alternative n
	  -- advantages
	  -- disadvantages
		- alternative n
		  -- advantages
		  -- disadvantages
			- alternative n
			  -- advantages
			  -- disadvantages

Figure 1.3

Need for Alternative Solutions to Separate Problems
Not Alternative Consideration of Several Problems

CHAPTER 2
DOCUMENTATION OF A CASE PROBLEM SOLUTION

The purpose of documentation is to communicate, and you should keep this in mind when preparing a written report of your case solution. While it might be appealing to present your material in an eloquent or technical way, a direct, easy-to-understand style is always the best approach.

Your instructor will probably want to see evidence of material that you have learned in the course. However, you should not include material that has no bearing on the problem at hand. Your instructor will only recognize this as an effort to pad the report, and this will only hurt your cause.

PREPARATION OF THE REPORT

You should plan your report in advance in order to allow enough time for each step. There are four basic steps, and none should be omitted.

Step 1--Write the Rough Draft

There are very few people who can prepare an acceptable piece of written work on their first effort. The authors of this *Casebook* are not among this select few. Most writers must refine the copy through a repetitive process. This is where word processing comes into play; it enables you to easily make changes until everything is just right.

In preparing the report, your first objective is to "get something down on paper." The idea is to record your thoughts and suggestions so that they can be viewed in their entirety. At the beginning, do not worry about sentence structure and choice of words. Those are important considerations that can wait until later.

Assuming that you have a report format to follow (an example is included in this chapter), the initial documentation effort is one of recording your material in the outline to produce a rough draft. If you follow the approach suggested in the previous chapter of making notes while the case is being studied, this step of preparing the rough draft becomes a process of converting the notes into a narrative.

Step 2--Refine the Rough Draft

Once you feel that you have recorded all of the material that bears on the problem, you review and refine the rough draft to assure the contents are presented in a logical and orderly manner and at the right level of detail.

A technique that contributes to the logical presentation will be described later in this chapter. The treatment of the material on the right level of detail can be achieved if you will put yourself in the position of a consultant who is preparing a report for the chief executive. Your task is to communicate the right amount of information so that the executive can solve the problem. If the report is too short, the executive will not have sufficient information for judging the report. If the report is too long, the executive may lose interest and either fail to read all of it or be unable to pick out the important points.

Eliminate grammatical errors such as misspelling, faulty punctuation, and incomplete sentences during your editing process. Every word that arouses doubt should be looked up in the dictionary or checked with the word processor's spelling checker. It might not seem important to correct errors like misspelled words or faulty punctuation. After all, this is a course in information systems, not English. However, any errors break the reader's train of thought and this interruption reduces your chances of receiving a good grade. The effort you put into grammar and spelling reflects the effort in your problem solution.

Step 3--Type the Report

If you do your own keyboarding, your final version of the rough draft becomes the report. If you plan for someone else do the keyboarding, a separate effort must be devoted to getting the material ready for the other person. The draft must be legible and all instructions should be clearly explained in writing. Most professional typists and word processing operators will gladly tell you what they need in order to meet your expectations of a high quality piece of work. You will probably use secretarial staff once you begin work and the secretary can tell you what is needed for reports.

Step 4--Proofread the Typed Report

Our experience as instructors has taught us that if a student is to skip over one of the four steps of report preparation, this is most likely to be it. In the rush to meet the deadline, it is tempting to assume that the report is exactly what you intended and not give it a final reading.

There is a good chance that the report is deficient in some way, especially when another person prepares the final copy. A mistake might have been made--either accidentally or because of poor instructions. Since you are the only one who knows what the final product should be, only you can put the final seal of approval on the paper. This requirement of a final review also holds true when you do your own keyboarding.

You are always responsible for proofreading your work.

Physical Specifications

Your instructor should answer the following questions:

1. Is the report to be typed?
2. If so, is it to be single- or double-spaced?
3. If a word processor is to be used, should the report be turned in on diskette or on paper?
4. If the report is on paper, how should the report be assembled--should it be bound, in a folder, or simply stapled?
5. Should there be a cover sheet?
6. Should you identify yourself by name or should you use your student number?

Regardless of the answers to these questions, you should make certain the report meets the quality standards of a business document. The reader should be able to easily read the report and to gain the full benefit from its analysis. This is difficult to do when the report is assembled improperly--pages are upside down or backwards, and folded pages are stapled shut.

You should make one final check of the report after it has been put together.

SUGGESTED REPORT FORMAT

A format that the authors have found to work well is offered here for consideration.

Report Heading

One approach is to simply place the heading at the top of the first page of the report. This is illustrated in Figure 2.1. Another approach is to include the same material on a cover sheet.

Report Sections

We recognized in Chapter 1 that the report sequence does not parallel the steps that you follow in solving the problem. In solving the problem, you assemble the evidence before reaching a solution decision. In preparing the report, you present the decision at the beginning, followed by the supporting evidence.

The five sections of the report format that we recommend are:

* Summary of Important Facts (including a brief description of the decision)
* Problem
* Decision
* Analysis
* Conclusion

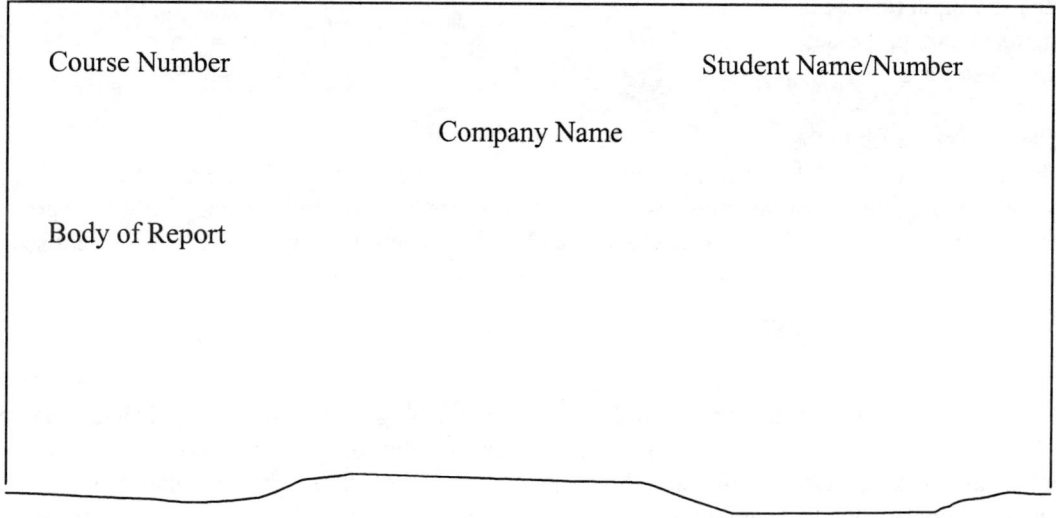

Figure 2.1

A Suggested Report Heading

Note the similarity to a newspaper article where the headline and the first few paragraphs convey the important points of the story. Information included toward the end of the article is more detailed and only supports or expands on what has already been said. This same technique is applicable to business reports in that it enables the reader to glean the important points up front without having to wade through the details at the rear.

Summary of Important Facts

It might seem like a waste of time to summarize a case situation that your instructor already understands inside and out. However, the purpose of the section is to not benefit the instructor, but to benefit you. The purpose is to ensure that you have read the case and understand it.

A key step in the systems approach is the gathering of data that bears on the problem. In a case problem, you gather this data by reading the case, understanding it, and extracting those key points that provide a good description of the situation. If you can summarize a case into a few concise statements, then your instructor will accept the fact that you have satisfactorily performed your data gathering.

Do not simply extract sentences from the case when summarizing the important points. Synthesize these points into comprehensive statements that relate directly to the problem. If material has no relation to the problem, it has no place in this section--no matter how interesting it might seem.

Whenever possible, inject your interpretation of the situation. Be careful not to get into the problem area(s), as that is the purpose of the next section. However, if there are characteristics of the situation that deserve comment, but fall outside the main problem area, you should include those remarks here.

This is a good place to eliminate minor problem areas from consideration. As an example, the main problem may be poor organization structure, yet less-important problems exist in the management and information systems areas. The secondary problems might be recognized and dismissed in this section so that the focus of the analysis can remain on the main area. Consider using a subheading for secondary problems.

Since the systems approach is to be followed in problem solution, the important facts can be presented as they relate to systems levels and parts. The subheadings accomplishing this are:

* The firm's environment
* Objectives and/or standards
* Outputs

11

* Management and organization structure
* Information processor
* Inputs and input resources
* Transformation processes
* Output resources

Any items that are not pertinent to the problem can be omitted.

You should make an effort to limit the summary of important facts to approximately two-thirds of a page. All estimates of page size assume that the report is typed, single-spaced with double spacing between paragraphs. A longer summary will indicate an inefficient data analysis and will also detract from the more important sections that follow.

Problem

When you correctly identify the problem, the task of describing it should not be difficult. Describe the problem in such a manner that it can be solved. There is a real possibility of hindering problem solution when you describe several problems rather than a single one. It would be difficult to address the advantages and disadvantages of the alternative solutions of each problem within the scope of the expected report.

Do not attempt to solve the problem in this section--simply describe it in clear and precise terms. The best approach is to begin with "The main problem is . . ." You can also use this section to briefly describe the effects of the problem(s) on the firm, and to identify related problems.

The problem section of the report will typically require no more than one-half of a page.

Logical Integration. Earlier in the chapter, we recognized that it is important that the material be presented in a logical manner. Three elements in the report must have this logical integration. These elements are the (1) problem definition, (2) alternatives, and (3) decision. This integration is illustrated in Figure 2.2.

The problem requires that several alternative solutions be considered, and the best solution becomes the decision. Since each of these elements are treated in separate sections of the report (the alternatives are described in the analysis section), these sections must express this interrelation. When you discuss your decision in the next section, relate it to the problem that you have defined. Do the same in the analysis section when you discuss the alternatives.

Decision

Keep your role of consultant in mind when preparing this section. Your decision becomes your recommendation to the manager of the system with the problem. This decision should be stated clearly. Do not embellish it with reasons why it should be done or the details of how to do it. That information comes later.

There should be a decision for each problem that has been identified. This is another reason for keeping the number of problems to a minimum. If three problems were identified in the previous section, and they were numbered, then the three corresponding decisions should be numbered accordingly. Do not simply rely on the numbering to relate the decision to the problem, and make certain that the reader knows which problem is being solved by which decision.

No more than one or two sentences should be required to state the solution to a single problem. Additional space can be used to briefly explain how the decision will solve the problem. This section should require about one-half of a page.

Analysis

If your instructor believes that the most important end product of a case study is the decision, and not necessarily how you reach it, then the decision section is the most important one in the report. The analysis section is the most important if your instructor places the most emphasis on the process that you follow in reaching the decision. Perhaps your instructor will place greater emphasis on the process during the beginning of the term as the systems approach is being learned, and more emphasis on the decision during the later weeks.

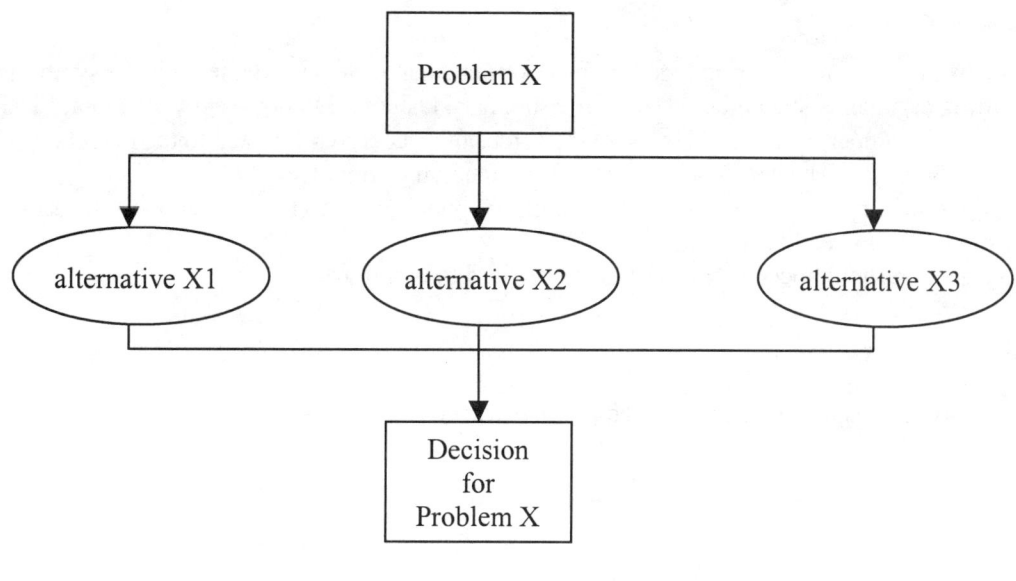

Figure 2.2

Interrelation of Problem, Alternatives, and Decision

The analysis section must provide the detailed support for the decision. This is where the alternatives are evaluated. Each feasible alternative for each problem must be evaluated--in terms of both its advantages and disadvantages. Just as in the previous section, there should be no question about which alternatives correspond to which problems and which decisions. Both the numbering of sections and the description of the alternatives should provide this interrelationship.

If you make any assumptions in solving the problem, this is the best place to include them. You can shape the direction of your solution and analysis by the assumptions you make. Do not hesitate to make assumptions since they generally indicate that you have given much thought to the problem and have realized that additional specifications are necessary in order to reach an acceptable solution. Be certain that your assumptions are realistic and are supported by the content and tone of the case. The assumptions may be listed separately, or they may be integrated into the narrative.

If it has been necessary for you to perform some data analysis, those facts should be presented in a form that is easily understood. As a general rule, figures and tables lend to the credibility of a report, but you should never include them without referencing them in the narrative.

Since your task is to convince the reader that your decision is a good one, your arguments must be strong and convey a confidence that your analysis is thorough and accurate. Use of superlatives is not the way to accomplish this. Phrases such as "tremendous cost savings" and "fantastic improvements in efficiency" are empty rhetoric. If cost savings will accrue, state exactly what they are. If efficiency will increase, state exactly in what sense. If you cannot provide objective measures, the reader becomes less certain that benefits will be achieved. The use of data and references from the literature, rather than superlatives, provides the support needed for your decision. This is where research outside the case material pays off. Do not neglect your textbook as a source of supporting material. Chances are it contains concepts or examples that support your analysis.

Ask yourself these questions after you have described your decision and the analysis supporting it:

1. Did I solve the problem(s) that I identified?
2. Did I support each decision in the most effective manner possible, considering the facts with which I had to work?

If the answer is "Yes" to both questions, you have completed your analysis and can conclude the effort with the final section. If not, you started writing the report too soon and should backtrack and rebuild your case.

The analysis should occupy the majority of the space in the report--generally one and one-half to two and one-half pages, not including tables or figures.

Conclusion

The main purpose of this section is to bring together the key points that have been made. It is the synthesis of all your work, and supporting arguments should be restated in a summary fashion. Do not simply state that "The arguments above support this as the proper decision." This wording forces the reader to refer back to the main body of the report to understand what you mean. The conclusion section must stand on its own feet.

This is where the brief implementation plan should be presented. A good format is to list each of the basic implementation steps. Try to keep the list short.

This final section should occupy no more than one-third to two-thirds of a page.

Report Length

Your report will be from three to four single-spaced pages if you conform to the estimates of page space given above.

CHAPTER 3
A SAMPLE CASE PROBLEM

Learning how to solve a business problem is like learning how to drive a car. You can read all of the driver's education manuals in the world, but sooner or later you must get out on the road. In the same way, you can read all of the textbook and case advice about problem solving, but eventually you must practice what you've read.

Your first effort in solving a business problem will likely be an uncertain one--just like the time mom or dad first let you get behind the wheel of the family car. But each time you repeat the process you get better at it.

The purpose of this chapter is to provide you with an opportunity to sharpen your skills, applying the material you learned in the first two chapters to a sample case problem. Study the problem and formulate a solution, applying the approach described in the first chapter. Be prepared to report your findings in the manner specified by your instructor. Chapter 4 provides an example of how the solution is formulated, and Chapter 5 consists of a sample written report of the solution using the format that was explained in Chapter 2.

THE ORANGE CLOCKWORKS COMPANY

The Orange Clockworks Company (OCC) was founded in Orange County, California in 1932 by Elijah Patterson. Patterson had worked on watches and clocks since he was a boy, and decided that he could make a better watch than those on the market. His intuition proved right and the "Orange" clock gained a reputation for reliability at a reasonable price. The scale of operations grew, and before long OCC was one of the world leaders in the manufacture of wind-up alarm clocks. One winding enabled the clock to run for seven days without stopping.

During the 1950s OCC developed a capability to produce electric clocks and added a variety of models to its line. The electric clock was so successful that the wind-up clocks were withdrawn from the United States market and produced only for underdeveloped countries where there was little electrical power.

OCC used punched card machines for data processing in the 1950s. In the 1960s, OCC executives decided they did not want OCC to acquire its own hardware and all of the other responsibilities that went with it, so they farmed out the data processing function to computer service bureaus. In 1985, the executives finally decided to hop on the computer bandwagon. Earnest Barnett was hired as the director of data processing. He reported to Bill Stuart, the vice president of finance. That superior-subordinate relationship still exists. One of Barnett's first actions was to install an IBM small business computer. Today, after a succession of system upgrades leading to the currently installed IBM minicomputer, the computer applications include:

* Payroll
* Inventory control (finished products)
* Billing
* Accounts receivable
* General ledger
* Financial statements
* Sales analysis

The computer calculates payroll amounts and prints the checks. At the end of the year, W-2 forms are printed showing annual income and tax figures. Employees use the forms in preparing their income tax returns. The computer also produces tax reports for the government.

The inventory of finished products is maintained on a disk file. There is one record in the disk file (the file is not part of a database) for each of the 225 different types of clocks. A record is updated each time the quantity is increased by production or decreased by sales. At the end of each month, the file is listed (one line is printed for each record), showing the value of the finished product inventory. The computer multiplies the on-hand balance for each item by its unit cost. The accounting department uses this information to prepare such monthly financial reports as the balance sheet and income statement.

A record is keyed into the computer for each type of clock that a customer orders. The record contains a code identifying the customer and a code identifying the clock. The quantity ordered is also entered. These order records are processed against the inventory file to reduce the item on-hand balances, and are then merged with customer name and address records in preparation for the invoicing operation. During invoicing, the computer prepares a record for each invoice that is used to update the accounts receivable file.

The appropriate records are deleted from the accounts receivable file when customers make payments. Records remaining in the file represent OCC's receivables, and each month the computer prints a listing of all the records. The credit manager uses this report to follow up on past-due customer payments by scanning the invoice date column to pick out those receivables over thirty days old.

The customer order records used in the billing operation are held until the end of the month. Then they are sorted into three different sequences to prepare reports showing sales by salesperson, sales by customer, and sales by product. These reports are sent to Sally James, the vice president of marketing. James does not use the reports since they were ordered by her predecessor and James sees no value in them. When James receives the reports, she tosses them in the wastebasket.

Sales and profits for OCC increased at a steady rate for many years. In the early 1990s sales started to slip. At first, management thought the problem was the economy. However, as the economy recovered over the next three years it became evident that OCC was losing its share of the alarm clock market. Salespersons calling on OCC customers (department stores, drug stores, and supermarkets) began complaining of stiffer competition. Customers had turned their attention to such other products as clock radios. Although the OCC alarm clock was less expensive than the clock radio, the clock radio was cheaper than a clock and a radio bought separately.

Annual revenue was predicted to be $22 million in 1993. However, actual 1993 sales were $17 million--$5 million less than the projection.

Additional salespersons were hired and the commission rates were increased in an effort to increase sales. These actions had little effect and in 1994, sales dropped to $16 million. There was no doubt about it--OCC's sales momentum was winding down.

When the 1994 results were made known to OCC management (about six weeks after the year end), a special management meeting was called. In attendance were J. L. Patterson, Bill Stuart, Sally James, and Jim Casey. Patterson is the grandson of the founder and his family controls approximately 80 percent of the firm's stock. He is also the president and chief executive officer. Jim Casey is the vice president of manufacturing.

J. L. Patterson: The figures for 1994 are in and they don't look good. It doesn't take an economic genius to see that we are in trouble--big trouble. The market for clocks changed and we stood by and did nothing. We are stuck with a product line that is, for lack of a better word, prehistoric. As CEO, I must take full responsibility for what has happened but I have looked to you for guidance in the past and I look to you now. We are all in this together. How did we get in such a situation? Sally?

Sally James: I think its due to two things. One, we haven't been able to promote our products the way our competitors do, and, second, we don't have competitive products. J. L., I've been trying to convince you for years to give us money in our budget for national TV ads. Our competitors spend millions, and that investment has paid off. The market place has been conditioned to believe that the way to wake up in the morning is to soft music from a clock radio--not the loud buzz of an alarm clock. The only time someone buys an alarm clock these days is for travel, and portable clock radios are beginning to cut into that market.

We have been a leader in the clock industry but now we find ourselves competing in the electronics industry, and that's a high stakes arena. There is no way we can keep OCC afloat without some new products. Give our sales reps some clock radios and we'll get back in gear. I'm not going to take the blame for our lost sales. Jim, why don't you explain why research and development hasn't kept us up with the market? Sometimes I wonder if we really have an R & D operation.

Jim Casey: Wait a minute, Sally. You know that this company has never pushed R & D. I have only two people for that work and they have their hands full just making the cosmetic changes that marketing requests. R & D isn't something that you create overnight. If you think we need a better R & D effort, then it's going to take some time and money. Manufacturing is not going to take the rap. Our ratio of cost of goods manufactured to sales has never been better. When marketing sells the products, OCC can produce them at a handsome profit. Sally, it seems to me that you don't know your territory--and that's marketing's responsibility, not mine.

J. L. Patterson: Bill, what do you have to say?

Bill Stuart: Finance is not the problem. That's not altogether true. We can get financing when we know ahead of time we need it. OCC has a superior credit rating with all of the local lending institutions. If we haven't had enough funds, it's because finance didn't know what we needed. I can't accept lack of money as our problem. I believe that it goes deeper than that. You recall that three years ago I established a planning group within finance. Our task was to look into the future five, six, or maybe ten years to anticipate where OCC was headed so as to determine our money needs. We quickly learned that we couldn't effectively make that projection without the cooperation of marketing and manufacturing. When that cooperation never came, we had to back off our original idea of long-range planning and just be concerned with the coming year.

Sally James: That's the first time I've heard that story.

Jim Casey: Me too.

Bill Stuart: Well, its true. In terms of short-range planning, we're doing an excellent job. I have some very good planners. But without the inputs from marketing and manufacturing, we can't see beyond the current year. I think we have some serious problems that must be solved if OCC expects to remain profitable.

J. L. Patterson: Bill, you might be right. In fact, all of you may be right. So, what do we do?

END-OF-CASE QUESTIONS

Each of the cases in the *Casebook* includes a list of questions at the end. Your instructor may prefer that you limit your problem solving to answering the questions. Since the purpose of the sample case is to demonstrate the use of the systems approach, the end-of-case questions are omitted here. The next chapter describes the process of solving the OCC problem using the systems approach.

CHAPTER 4
SOLUTION OF THE SAMPLE PROBLEM

We suggested in Chapter 1 that you make notes in a certain format when the case is being studied. The format that we recommend includes a page for each of the system levels or parts. A set of six completed forms is included at the end of this chapter to illustrate how this note-making process can be accomplished. Refer to the forms as they are discussed. Blank forms are included for each case problem in this casebook. Your instructor will advise you whether to use the forms, and whether to turn them in as evidence of your analysis.

A key point for you to understand about the forms is the fact that they are working papers. Unless your instructor tells you otherwise, do not make a special effort to make them especially neat.

Form 1--The Problem Setting

Form 1 addresses the setting for solving the problem, keying on the firm's environment and important facts. The upper half of the form is devoted to the environment and the lower half to the facts.

When addressing the environment, consider the elements that were identified earlier in the Figure 1.1 diagram. List each element that you believe has some influence on the problem and include a brief explanation.

Use the remainder of the form to list any facts relating to the firm that you feel to be worth noting at the time of the first reading.

Form 2--The Firm

Form 2 is concerned with the elements of the system of the firm. The seven system elements appear in the order of their problem-solving hierarchy. As with Form 1, the notes you enter are simply important points and are not intended to be problems. The purpose of this form is to sort out the facts relating to the firm.

Form 3--The Firm's Subsystems

Form 3 enables you to address the subsystems of the firm. There are four blank sections that you use to make notes relating to subsystems. It is left to you to determine what the subsystems represent. In the OCC example they are the functional areas of the organization--marketing, manufacturing, and finance. They could be management levels, geographic areas, product lines, and so on. Be certain that you identify each subsystem area of the form, as is done in the example with the functional area names.

You complete the first three forms as you read the case for the first time. This accomplishes the data-gathering step of the systems approach. Then, digest the data. Think about it. Ask yourself: "What is causing this situation?" This thought process will lead you down the symptom chain to the root cause.

Form 4--Symptoms and Problems

Use Form 4 to keep track of symptoms and problems. List them in the upper areas. There are separate blanks for the environment, objectives and/or standards, output, management, and the information processor. The inputs and elements of the physical system are combined in a single area.

Analyze the entries to determine which are problems and which are symptoms. Does one cause another? In the sample case, inferior management practices can be identified as the cause of poor objectives, obsolete output, extreme functionalism existing within the firm, and lack of a real information system. There does not appear to be anything wrong with the physical system. At the bottom of the form, the most important problem is identified--inability of top-level management to develop a long-range plan. A functional management attitude is identified as a secondary problem. In order for the firm to solve its problem it must come up with a long-range planning capability.

In evaluating a firm's management team, there are times when it cannot be criticized for failing to act or acting in the wrong manner. In some companies, especially small ones that are growing rapidly, managers are overworked and must attend to only the most pressing matters. You will have to determine if such is the situation in each case. From the information in the OCC case, it does not appear that the managers are overworked.

Form 5--Solution Alternatives

With the problem or problems identified at the bottom of Form 4, the different alternatives to problem solution can be noted on Form 5. In the sample case these are the different ways that OCC can go about long-range planning. If you have identified multiple problems or have a lengthy list of advantages and disadvantages, you will need to make multiple copies of the form.

Notice the numbering system that is used in the sample to organize the alternatives, their advantages, and their disadvantages. As a general rule, presenting this material in such an outline makes it easier to read than if you use paragraphs.

In identifying the alternatives, think in terms of <u>what</u> is to be done and <u>who</u> is to do it, but do not view the alternatives narrowly in terms of whether to do the work internally or hire an outside consultant. <u>Any</u> case problem can be addressed in such a superficial way, and your instructor wants you to dig much deeper. In the sample case, OCC has three main choices in attaining a long-range planning capability. They can form a separate planning division, they can let finance do it, and they can form an executive planning committee. Each has its advantages and disadvantages.

Form 6--The Decision and Its Implementation

Use your judgment to select the best alternative, and identify your decision on Form 6. This should be a brief statement, perhaps no more than two or three sentences. Finally, think about how the firm can implement your decision. What resources will be required? What steps should be taken?

Now you have solved the case problem. The remaining task is to report the solution. The next chapter contains a sample.

McLeod / Schell Case Solution Form 1
The Problem Setting

Case: Orange Clockworks Company Name: _____

Environmental Elements:

Customers prefer competition's clock radios.

Paterson family is a majority stockholder.

Competition is from firms in the electronics industry.

OCC has good credit rating in the financial industry.

Important Facts:

Computer operations began in 1985. Consists of mostly data processing applications.

DP director is Earnest Barnett.

Sales began to drop in early 1990s. Prehistoric product line.

Never pushed R & D.

McLeod / Schell Case Solution Form 2
Elements of the Firm as a System

Case: **Orange Clockworks Company** Name: _____

Objectives and/or Standards:

OCC doesn't seem to have any. If so, they are sales projections based upon past history. Long-range planning fell flat when marketing and manufacturing failed to cooperate. Good basis for short-term planning.

Output:

Decreasing sales due to shift of customer demand to different products. Products not innovative; only kept alive by making cosmetic changes. OCC has not kept pace.

Management and Organization:

Functional organization. Much finger-pointing by vice presidents. Need for better communication at executive level.

Information Processor:

Computer used mainly for data processing. Printouts given to Accounting are used to prepare financial reports. Credit manager uses past-due receivables report. Marketing VP doesn't use sales analysis reports. Annual reports are late.

Inputs and Input Resources:

No deficiencies here.

Transformation Process:

Manufacturing operation is very efficient -- low cost of goods manufactured.

Output Resources:

No problems.

McLeod / Schell Case Solution Form 3
Subsystems of the Firm

Case: Orange Clockworks Company   Name: _____

Subsystem: Marketing

Doesn't keep up with customers' needs. Seems like there is a lack of formal information feedback from the market place. Strong functional attitude; quick to blame manufacturing.

Subsystem: Manufacturing

Operation should be efficient because product line is narrow and seldom changes.

Doesn't seem to recognize importance of good R & D.

Has the same functional attitude as marketing.

Subsystem: Finance

Has built good credit rating.

Didn't push long-range planning.

VP not a good communicator at the executive level.

Subsystem:

McLeod / Schell Case Solution Form 4
Problems and Symptoms

Case: Orange Clockworks Company   Name: _____

Environment: Stiff competition
Objectives and/or Standards: No long-range plan
Output: Obsolete product line
Management and Organization: Functional attitude, poor communication
Information Processor: Used for data processing, with some report outputs
Inputs and Physical System: Manufacturing operation operates at low cost

Main Problem(s):

1. Inability of top-level management to plan

2. Functional management attitude

3.

McLeod / Schell Case Solution Form 5
Alternatives

Case: Orange Clockworks Company   Name: _____

Alternative: Form executive committee consisting of top execs

Advantages:

1. Execs know the business
2. Planning would have total-company focus

Disadvantages:

1. Execs might not have the right planning skills
2. Execs might not have enough time

Alternative: Let Finance division do planning

Advantages:

1. Planning staff already in place
2. Low start-up costs

Disadvantages:

1. Planning might favor Finance function

McLeod / Schell Case Solution Form 5
Alternatives

Case: Orange Clockworks Company   Name: _____

Alternative: Form planning division that reports to executive committee

Advantages:

1. Professional planners
2. Full-time planning job
3. Place in organization would ensure total-company focus, not functional focus
4. Could build on current planning staff

Disadvantages:

1. Planners might not have good knowledge of the company and its products
2. Planners would be expensive

Alternative:

Advantages:

Disadvantages:

McLeod / Schell Case Solution Form 6
Decision and Implementation

Case: **Orange Clockworks Company**   Name: _____

Decision:

Form a planning division of professional planners reporting to the executive committee.

Implementation Resources Needed:

Additional planning personnel

Computer support in the form of planning software and perhaps hardware

Training program to orient new planners to the company, its products, and its markets

Implementation Steps to be Followed:

1. Hire a manager of the planning division
2. Transfer planners from Finance
3. Hire additional planners as needed
4. Conduct company training program
5. Obtain needed computer resources
6. Establish procedure for planning -- gathering data and reporting results to top management
7. Put planning system into operation

CHAPTER 5
A SAMPLE SOLUTION

As you report your solution, do not be afraid that you will fail to identify the <u>single answer</u> that your instructor is expecting. A case problem would have to be extremely simple to be solved in only one way. The Orange Clockworks case is not complex but each problem-solver's solution will likely be unique in some way.

Your instructor will want to see evidence of the following accomplishments in your report:

1. You understand the case situation.
2. You have searched for problem causes and not settled for symptoms.
3. You have identified the problem in a top-down, systematic fashion.
4. You have considered different ways to solve the problem.
5. You have evaluated the alternatives by examining both advantages and disadvantages.
6. The alternative that you selected as the solution is the best way to solve the problem that you identified.
7. Your solution can be implemented, and you have given thought to how that can be accomplished in the case firm.

If your report reveals these accomplishments, you should not worry about your decision. It may not be exactly the same one that your instructor develops, but you did your best with the resources you had available. No instructor, or employer, should expect anything more.

The case approach can be an exciting way to learn, but it demands time and effort. You will get out of it exactly what you put in. As you work on each case, keep in mind that the technique you are learning is one that you will put to good use as you pursue your career. The time you put in now will pay off in your future. Study the example report below.

Class: Business 301   **Date: August 22, 2000**

Orange Clockworks Company

Summary of Important Facts

Orange Clockworks Company (OCC) is losing its position of market leadership. Sales leveled off in the early 1990s after a history of steady increase. Actual sales in 1993 were $5 million less than the $22 million projected. The condition worsened in 1994 when sales dipped another $1 million. OCC executives see the cause as a trend away from alarm clocks to clock radios. OCC did not become aware of the trend until they had lost their market position. The vice president of marketing blames the lost sales on an inadequate marketing budget and lack of R & D by manufacturing. The vice president of manufacturing claims that marketing did not understand their customers well enough to anticipate their needs. The vice president of finance does not believe the problem to be a lack of money. Rather, he mentions the difficulty that finance had in working with the other functions in long-range planning.

Problem

The problem is the lack of a long-range planning activity within OCC. This problem seems to be caused primarily by an inability of the president and the vice presidents of marketing and manufacturing to see the importance of such planning.

Lack of communication among the executives is also a factor. The vice presidents of marketing and manufacturing do not seem to work well together, and the vice president of finance apparently never communicated to the other executives the problems that were encountered when the attempt at long-range planning failed.

Lack of a long-range plan has resulted in a lack of objectives and performance standards for the OCC organization. OCC has no yardstick against which to measure its own performance other than sales volume and such financial measures as cost of goods manufactured.

The use of computing is another condition within OCC worth noting. The computer applications are limited to data processing and there is no evidence that computer systems have been developed to meet specific information needs of managers. For example, the credit manager must pour over a listing of receivables, picking out the exceptions. The computer could well perform this selection. In the case of the vice president of marketing, her computer reports (the ones specified by a previous manager) are not being used. Top management does not seem aware of the poor level of support that is being provided by the computer unit, and of the potential support that is possible.

Decision

The OCC president should immediately take two actions. First, he should make it clear to the members of the executive committee that they have responsibility for strategic planning and control and that they will formally address this issue on a periodic basis, such as weekly or monthly. Second, OCC should establish a planning division, consisting of professional planners and a support staff, reporting directly to the executive committee.

The task of the planning division will be to work with the executives in developing the strategic plans. The executives should guide this procedure by specifying when planning is to be done, how far into the future the planning horizon should go, and how information is to be reported.

The first strategic plan should be based on a marketing research study aimed at identifying long-term consumer needs in the clock and clock radio markets. Subsequent research studies will keep the market information current. As the strategic planning unit develops more current information, the executives will revise the long-range plan accordingly. In this way, OCC will continually monitor its position in its competitive environment and will have an appropriate plan to guide its operations.

The planning division should make use of all techniques and resources, including those utilizing computer-based planning systems.

Analysis

President Patterson has three basic choices in how OCC will go about its strategic planning. Either he and the other executives can do it themselves (alternative 1 discussed below), they can let the finance division do it (alternative 2), or they can establish a special planning division (alternative 3). Alternative 2 assumes that if finance does the planning they can count on better cooperation than they received previously.

Alternative 1--Form an executive planning committee consisting of the president and vice presidents. The committee would devote time on a scheduled basis to developing the plan and evaluating actual performance compared to the plan.

The **advantages** of forming an executive planning committee are:

1. The executives know the business better than anyone else, assuring that the plan reflects where they want the firm to go.
2. The planning would have a total-company focus. This assumes that president Patterson has a strong influence on the committee's actions and that the vice presidents work together.

The **disadvantages** of forming an executive planning committee are:

1. The executives may not have the necessary planning skills. There is nothing in the case to indicate that the executives know how to plan.
2. The executives may not have enough time to do a good planning job. As OCC tries to head off its sales decline, the executives will have many other distractions.

Alternative 2--Give the finance division the planning responsibility and provide the necessary resources to do a good job.

The **advantages** of letting finance do the forecasting are:

1. A staff of planners currently exists in the finance division. It is assumed that they have the necessary knowledge and skills. Perhaps additional staff will be needed, but a nucleus is already in place.
2. Since a planning staff is present, the start-up costs of establishing such a group have already been incurred.

A **disadvantage** of letting finance do the forecasting is:

1. Since the planners are a part of finance, they may show preferential treatment to finance in the planning process. There is a good chance that planning will not have a total-company focus.

Alternative 3--Form a planning division that reports directly to an executive committee.

The **advantages** of forming a planning division that reports to an executive committee are:

1. Planning would be done by professional planners who are skilled in the necessary techniques.
2. The planners would devote full time to planning, and this would free the executives and other managers from much of the time-consuming data gathering and analysis.
3. By reporting to an executive committee, a total-company focus would be assured.
4. Most or all of the current planning staff could be transferred from finance to the new group, minimizing the start-up costs.

The **disadvantages** of forming a top-level planning division are:

1. Professional planners would not know as much about the business as would line managers such as the president and vice presidents.
2. In terms of out-of-pocket costs, the expense of maintaining a separate planning unit would be greater than letting the executives take on the work as an added responsibility. However, if the executives devote their valuable time to the mechanics of planning, the real cost could well be higher.

The establishment of a professional planning group that would have a total-company focus (alternative 3) appears to be the best solution. The existence of such a group would free the executives from much of the time-consuming work that goes into developing and maintaining a long-range plan, and would allow time for other duties. The executives, however, would still be involved in the planning process. There would have to be a high level of communication between the executives, other managers, and planners in order to ensure a good plan.

Conclusion

OCC sales are $5 to $6 million less than predicted and the problem appears to be getting worse. Patterson must recognize that he and his fellow executives have done a poor job of staying in touch with their market and developing plans that ensure OCC has products that the customers need. Patterson must also recognize that serious flaws exist within OCC in terms of communication between the functions and in the level of support provided by the computer unit. An integral part of the solution to the planning problem will be the achievement of improved internal communication and cooperation as well as an expansion of the computer applications to include decision support.

In implementing the solution, the following steps should be taken:

1. Patterson should form the executive committee.
2. The executive committee should establish a separate planning division that consists of the current planners in the financial division.
3. The executive committee should work with the planning division to devise a procedure that spells out when annual plans will be prepared, the time horizon for the plan, and the means of reporting, the plan as well as performance against the plan to the responsible managers.

4. The executive committee should provide the planning division with the needed resources such as computer support. In the event that the OCC computer operation cannot respond immediately to the needs, such other options as outsourcing can be pursued on an interim basis.
5. The executive committee should charge the vice president of finance, Bill Stuart, with the responsibility of upgrading the computer applications to include decision support information to be used in planning and other management functions.

OCC must act now to make the transition from a firm with no real direction to one with a long-range plan and an organization to support that plan.

SOME OBSERVATIONS ON THE CASE SOLUTION

Earlier mention was made of the "tone" of the case. In evaluating a case situation you are guided not only by the words but also by how the words are woven together to provide the overall setting. This is the tone of the case.

The tone of the OCC case paints a picture of managers who get caught up in functional clashes but still seem to have the best interests of OCC at heart. Aside from the poor communication and absence of a planning capability, which are serious deficiencies, there is nothing to indicate that the managers should be replaced. The solution should therefore be based on salvaging the current management resource and building upon it. If the current managers prove to be incapable of the new level of performance, then more drastic action can be taken, but the first attempt should be to work within the existing management team.

When you were instructed to focus on only one system element, rather than multiple ones, the observation was made that management will invariably be involved. Such is the case with OCC. The system element that is deficient is the objectives and standards, and it is deficient because top management has failed to put that element in place. In order to overcome the system deficiency, top management must take action.

You recall that the objectives and/or standards element is the first one analyzed (Figure 1.2). It therefore takes precedence over any other elements in the system. The objectives problem must be solved before an attempt is made to solve any others. That is the reason why the deficiencies in R & D and the information system are not regarded as main problems. The R & D and computer problems cannot be completely solved until objectives and standards have been established. With a good strategic plan in place, top management most certainly will then focus on the R & D and computer support issues.

Note that costs are identified as disadvantages of two of the alternatives. However, specific figures are not included because the case provides nothing upon which to base cost estimates. We do not know from the information in the case how many planners will be needed, what their salaries will be, how many secretaries will be needed, how much computer software, and so on. The manner in which the cost issue is addressed is an example of how you tailor your analysis to fit the material in the case.

CASES

COUNCIL OF 100

The Council of 100 was formed in 1975 to help attract new businesses to Adams county. Florine was the largest city in the county with a population of over 200,000. The area had long been known for its small shipping port and forestry products. In fact, wood pulp and processed lumber accounted for 80% of the cargo being shipped from the port in 1975. The Council wanted to broaden the business base of the county by attracting small manufacturing and technology related businesses to the area.

The Council was originally made up of prominent business leaders in the county and people active in politics at the county and state level. The first priority of the Council was to improve transportation and communications into and out of the area. A campaign was begun to improve the airport facilities and to convince legislators that investments in road systems in the county would be good for economic growth in the entire state. The telephone company introduced inexpensive and fast Internet connections and provided a wide range of wireless communications options. This transportation portion of the campaign culminated in the mid-1980s when several state roads were widened to four-lane highways and the last extension of the interstate highway, which passed within five miles of Florine, was completed.

During the next 20 years the Council focused on luring businesses to the area that would hire relatively well-paid, well-educated employees. This strategy succeeded because the state enjoyed a national reputation for education in both grade schools and colleges. Since it is far less expensive to hire skilled employees who already live and/or go to school in the state, many businesses were attracted to Florine and to other cities in Adams county.

During the same period the state enjoyed higher economic growth than most of the nation and Adams county's growth was slightly higher than the state's. This situation suited the Council well because the growth increased property values, added tax monies to the treasury, and kept the area energetic with new ideas and progress. The Council's composition of business leaders and politicians served Adams county well because the greatest advantage in attracting new business during the first twenty years of the campaign was a network of personal contacts.

The Council of 100 was organized as a non-profit organization that had the unofficial blessing of both the city and county governments. Its organization structure consisted of a director, two assistant directors, an office manager, and several staff. The Council had a board of directors and there are approximately 100 board members at any given time. Hence the name, Council of 100.

Tracy Friedman has been the director for the last five years. She received her college degree in Business Administration and then remained in school another year to earn a second degree in Public Administration. She had worked as an assistant director for organizations similar to the Council of 100 for 12 years before she was hired as its director. She is responsible for all budget, personnel, and operating decisions of the Council.

The board of trustees of the Council has a chairman and committee chairmen for the three permanent committees: long range planning, fund raising, and public relations. Many ad hoc committees are formed to help attract a business to the area once a business has shown it is truly interested in locating in Adams county. Different members of the board make contacts with counterparts in that targeted business that perform similar job functions. Members of the board of directors who are purchasing agents would contact the purchasing agent of the targeted business. Personnel managers, production managers, and others in the business would also be contacted. The personal contacts by members of the Council's board of trustees provided a great deal of positive exposure for Adams county. The Council believed that the more the prospective business knew about Adams county, the more likely it would be to relocate there.

Peggy Mizell and George Fredrick are the assistant directors. They are responsible for identifying businesses that might be interested in relocating to Adams county. They make most of the initial contacts and perform most of the research that determines how good a match can be made between the needs of the business and the resources of the area. Both Peggy and George have been in this line of work for more than five years. Tracy generally becomes involved with prospective businesses only after they have shown an interest and ability to relocate to Adams county.

Finding prospective businesses and matching their needs to area resources requires great amounts of research on companies and the people that run them. In the past, members of the board of trustees acted as the source of most information, but during the last ten years most information came from publicly accessible sources: government databases, college alumni sources, trade associations, news services, and others.

For example, last year Wolfson Building Associates relocated to Florine. George had identified the company as a prospect by reviewing annual reports of a trade association that Wolfson Building had belonged to for many years. George noticed a pattern of turnover of key employees in the firm and also that Wolfson's contributions to the trade association had declined significantly. He investigated newspaper stories and local television reports that documented the cause of Wolfson's decline to be a lack of adequate access to interstate highways.

Wolfson Building had relied heavily upon rail transportation of its main products: prefabricated trusses for buildings and prefabricated interior walls. Unfortunately, Wolfson was located in a state where construction was slow. As the economy declined, the railroad providing service to Wolfson had scaled back operations and severely limited Wolfson's ability to ship its products in a timely manner. The business could not easily change to truck transportation since Wolfson was located more than 100 miles from the nearest interstate highway.

With this in mind George sought information on the construction industry in Adams county and the surrounding region. He found that home construction was moderately ahead of the national average and that construction of malls and office buildings (Wolfson's main type of customer) was far above national averages. It took George several weeks of going to libraries, reviewing records from county courthouses, and requesting industry statistics from governmental and trade association sources to gather the necessary information.

It took 18 months from the Council's first contact with Wolfson Building before the move was complete. More than 250 of the 372 employees were relocated to the Florine area. The remaining jobs were filled by Florine residents. Wolfson quickly began to flourish with easy access to both rail and highway transportation. The closer proximity to customers meant that Wolfson incurred less transportation costs and, therefore, higher profits. Since transportation costs were lower, Wolfson's products could be offered at a lower price and that led to more sales. Wolfson expanded production and hired 60 additional workers from the local community during its first year of operation in Florine.

The attraction of Wolfson to Florine is a classic example of how the Council works. George researched a wide variety of data sources to glean the information needed to match Wolfson needs with Adams county resources. Once the initial contacts with Wolfson were positive, Tracy searched real estate sources to identify possible locations for the manufacturing operations. She searched financial databases for real estate institutions specializing in locating a new property site while selling the old property at the same time. This was particularly important to Wolfson since it was financially unable to bear the costs of a new manufacturing location if it had to simultaneously make mortgage payments on the old site.

The work required to attract Wolfson is typical of the work performed by the Council staff. The staff is in the business of information. They have to know what information is needed and where to find it. During the last five years, information became increasingly computer accessible via networks. This meant that Tracy, George, and Peggy would have to become as skilled in using computer-based information sources as they already were with traditional searches of libraries and court records.

Tracy called a meeting to discuss the use of computer resources to redefine how they performed their job duties. Peggy and George would attend as well as Mary McCall (chairman of the board of trustees) and Robert Fiske (office manager).

Tracy Friedman: I've called this meeting to discuss how we can change our work habits in order to make us more efficient. We've moved from competing with other counties in the state to other states in the country and even to other countries. About 5% of the contacts we make are with businesses that currently have no operations within the United States. But our biggest source of clients are businesses in other states.

    About 60% of our clients are out of state, but usually in our region of the country. Our data gathering takes time since most of it is done by searching libraries and calling contacts in state agencies or trade associations. By then another city or state is trying to get our client to relocate where they are. In our business it's crucial to identify prospects and quickly provide them with information. We need to answer any question they have within a few days, certainly no longer than a week.

Mary McCall: Tracy and I have met with many of the people on the board of trustees and we feel the goals and mission of the Council have not changed. We want to identify and attract businesses to Adams county that utilize well-paid and well-educated employees. We want better than average growth when compared to the state and national figures, but not so much growth that we strain services such as schools, waste management systems, traffic, or other municipal services.

    More and more cities are starting to do what we have been doing for over twenty years. They've made it harder to compete for attractive businesses to locate or relocate in Adams county. The information they send out is very professional, a number of cities put out first rate materials on demand. Some are even using web sites.

    Wilmington, North Carolina has a site at http://www.wilmington-nc.org that provides a lot of information. It gives reasons to relocate, as well as web addresses of many businesses in the area so clients thinking of relocating can see what commerce is already in the area.

Tracy Friedman: We've got to be able to compete. That means we have to be quicker to find and attract businesses. And we must start producing glossy publications that are of as high a quality as any print shop can produce. We probably also need some web-based presence to attract clients. Especially since technology related businesses are one of our main targets. I mean, if we don't even have a web page what kind of impression are we making?

Peggy Mizell: We've seen many people in the business start using computer databases to track businesses and find information. Some use CD-ROM databases that the government or private companies put out. Others subscribe to online services that take your query and provide you with answers. But with those services you never get to see the data yourself, only the "answers" to your "questions." A lot of the time I really don't know exactly what I'm looking for until I see it.

George Fredrick: The county adopted a policy that makes records available by either computer access or manually looking up the records. Many counties across the country have the same policy. Computer access to Adams county records costs $100 per year. It's a flat fee with no additional charges based upon how many times you use it. All of the states use similar access, but the type of information you can access varies by state and even by county within the state.

   I think we can get the data we need using computer accessible methods. The only real problem I've heard of people having is that the number of years of data might be limited. For example, Adams county approved computerized access to records in 1991. Records from 1991 until now are accessible by computer but earlier records have to be manually retrieved.

Peggy Mizell: Many of the federal databases we've searched in libraries are computer accessible. But they require access to the Internet in order to get to the data.

Mary McCall: That shouldn't be a problem. There are commercial companies that provide access at a nominal cost. No matter how we gain access to the Internet it is going to be inexpensive to connect.

Robert Fiske: We need to look at what the information "highway" offers, but we should also take stock of what we're driving. Almost any computer can gain access to the Internet, but unless it has speed, storage space, and fast transmission speeds down the phone line, it won't be a satisfactory ride.

   For example, Peggy and George often get maps of counties or cities when they are doing their research. Those are graphical images that take a lot of transmission data and large amounts of disk storage space for storing the images. We don't have the equipment to take advantage of what is being offered. I get most of the maps I need at home on my own computer using the maps site at http://maps.yahoo.com and the maps show about everything I need. I don't use the computers here in the office because they're too slow.

   All of our microcomputers are IBM compatibles but they're six years old. They meet the minimum requirements for running the software we use now but the machines are not capable of tapping the potential you have been talking about. It's like riding a motor scooter when you need a jet.

Mary McCall: You're right. The reason that's the case is because office equipment for the Council has typically been donated by one or more of the businesses represented by the board of trustees. When Hood Industries changed to their new microcomputers they gave seven of their old ones to the Council and donated the rest to county high schools. That has also worked for the printers to go along with the microcomputers, photocopy machines, the fax machine, and most of the equipment in the office. Almost nothing is bought new.

   The Board realizes that in order to stay competitive it may have to assess its members a "technology fee" on a recurring basis in order to keep the Council's computer equipment in a competitive position. Another alternative is for a company to buy hardware and then loan it to the Council for a period of time, say two years, before taking it back.

   Some of the "borrowing" schemes seem attractive but there are some questions as to who is responsible in case of damage or theft. When you lend the hardware of a company you might be violating the contract agreement of one of the vendors. Different vendors have different types of contracts. That could create a legal hassle that makes many companies wary of sharing equipment. Besides, a lot of companies are so concerned about computer security that they don't want any non-employees accessing their computer resources.

My guess is that a technology fee of $100 will be assessed to each member of the Council. That fee may be assessed only every two or three years depending upon what equipment the Council needs.

Robert Fiske: That may not be enough. The $100 fee will yield about $10,000 for new equipment. My guess is that Tracy, Peggy, and George could use laptop computers so that they could access data and perform computing analyses with prospective businesses while they are away from the office. Three laptops, plus full-screen monitors and keyboards for use in the office, would cost around $9,000.

Then we'd need machines for the office staff. That would be four computers at a total price of maybe $8,000 to $10,000. We're already well beyond the amount of money the technology fee would generate. A three year turnover rate for computers would mean roughly $6,000 needed every three years for hardware but we also have to consider Internet connections, software, access to private databases, and other costs.

Mary McCall: But we could sell the current microcomputers and use that money to help buy new computers.

Robert Fiske: Used computers have very low values. In fact, a six year old PC has almost no value at all. Hardware requirements for new software packages generally exceed the hardware capabilities of PCs that old.

I know that seems drastic, but within eighteen months the power of a PC doubles in relationship to its cost. So if you spend $2,000 today on a computer then in eighteen months you could get one with twice the power for the same $2,000.

Tracy Friedman: Then what would we expect to spend for all of the computer hardware and software we need? And don't forget the costs for accessing the Internet.

Robert Fiske: I think we'd need $30,000 at a minimum. And we'd be spending that much every three years if we expect to compete with agencies that are trying to get businesses to locate to other areas. $10,000 from the Council's technology fee every two or three years won't be enough, we'd need at least that much each year. What you have to remember is that we've changed from competing against other councils and chambers of commerce within our state, we now compete with other states and some international groups. These groups have gotten sophisticated and computerized.

Tracy Friedman: We need a national and international focus if for no other reason than the fact that a shipping port is of no use to a business base that doesn't extend beyond the region. The same can be said for our airport facilities. I know that I tend to think of passenger flights when I think of the airport, but its air cargo revenues are three times as much as revenues generated by passengers.

Summers county [the most populous county in the state] took the position that they would make growth their measure of success for attracting businesses to the county. They would count the number of employees generated by attracting new businesses to the county as the one true measure of their efforts. Well, they have attracted more businesses and the number of employees in the county is larger than two years ago. But the total payroll has dropped because the types of jobs brought to Summers county are for unskilled workers. Our position is that we seek businesses that add value to Adams county and for which Adams county can provide value.

Peggy Mizell: Let's assume that we will acquire new computers and have access to databases on the Internet. What databases do we want to access?

George Fredrick: We can start with government databases that show retail sales, building permits, payroll taxes, and other public information. The information at www.census.gov is a bonanza. Every state government and most counties allow access by computers to their "public" databases. Then there are all of the news groups and discussion groups. Most of the trade organizations sponsor bulletin board service and keep a great deal of their information available through computer connections. Health care workers, communications workers, construction, hotel/restaurant management, and many others keep such lists. I've seen the telephone access numbers at the library so we can easily connect to their service.

Some of the companies we want to reach have electronic bulletin boards. You know Red Arrow Electronics, the firm in Hawaii that we've been in contact with? They have an electronic bulletin board and we've found out a great deal of information from it. We know how many employees they have, their geographic sales regions, the names and phone numbers of their senior managers, and many more facts. I wouldn't be surprised if many of the businesses we are interested in had such electronic bulletin boards.

Robert Fiske: Before we get too far from the hardware and software needs to access this information, let me see if I can recap what we want to have. We'll need PCs that are current, not "hand-me-downs" from a member business. Since we'll be getting a lot of information downloaded from these sites, we'll need a large hard drive for storage and maybe even a CD writer to make CDs to keep large data sets. The Internet can be the access medium for obtaining much information. We'll need new software to take advantage of the new hardware. And scanners, a digital camera, very fast Internet connections ...

Mary McCall: Wait a second. I don't know if we're ready to begin looking at a laundry list of equipment. Have we even decided that the equipment is really needed or if it is just wanted? I don't know if the board of trustees is going to raise the money it would take to get many new machines. We need to consider what is currently available and make a plan to acquire other resources as our budgets allow.

The equipment in the Council office can access all of the databases we've been talking about. They may not be fancy, but they certainly are better than what many companies in Florine use. We need to assess what capabilities we have with current equipment.

Tracy Friedman: Mary's right. But we also have to weigh the costs of the new equipment against the benefits of attracting new businesses to Adams county. Is it reasonable to believe we will attract technology-based businesses to our area if we don't have current technology to market ourselves to those businesses?

But let's not forget a major issue here, our method of doing our job has changed due to changes in technology. Is there an opportunity for us that we haven't discussed?

Peggy Mizell: I think we need to address the central issue: technology has redefined our job tasks. Opportunities exist to change the focus of how we perform our jobs, something more important than the issue of manually doing library searches versus computer access to databases. In the past we have gathered and analyzed data based upon the particular task we needed to complete. Data use was based on the function we were performing. With so much data available to us through electronic means we should consider letting the data we have available drive the functions we perform.

George Fredrick: You mean if we stumble upon a database of commercial fishing boats we should try to attract commercial fishing to the area?

Peggy Mizell: No, it's not like that. Let me explain it this way. We've always had a well defined goal: attract businesses to Adams county that add value to the community. The goal hasn't changed but the steps we take to accomplish the goal have changed dramatically.

We have been using the steps as a problem solving exercise. First, know the goal. Second, decide what decisions and/or tasks are required to reach the goal. Third, gather the information needed to support the decisions and tasks. That is a valid and very effective strategy.

Now we are in a different set of circumstances. We realize that the business of the Council is essentially an information business. Knowing who, what, where, and how are the critical success factors for us. We succeed or fail based upon our abilities to find good information.

Should we reorder the steps we take to reach our goals?

Tracy Friedman: What you're describing is called enterprise modeling. Organizations that identify information as a key corporate resource have been working with the concept you've described. Those companies are typically large, but the same principle applies to the Council even though we have only seven employees.

I think we need to study what we've talked about. We need more information about how we do our job and also the equipment we need to support what we do. Whether we take an enterprise modeling view or a traditional view, we know we must migrate to more sophisticated computing equipment if we want to stay competitive in attracting businesses to Adams county.

QUESTIONS:

1. The Council of 100 depends on information as its primary asset. How has the Internet changed the way the Council and other information intensive organizations perform their job tasks?

2. Many libraries and governmental agencies allow access to their databases from many organizations. Describe some of the benefits and some of the risks associated with allowing access to database information by an outside organization.

3. Most microcomputers function as well after five years as the first day they operated. Why should you replace microcomputers after a few years even though the equipment is mechanically and electronically sound?

4. Explain why the inexpensive, easy access to databases via the Internet should cause organizations to reconsider the role of marketing.

McLeod / Schell Case Solution Form 1
The Problem Setting

Case: <u>Council of 100</u>　　　　　　　　Name: _____

Environmental Elements:

Important Facts:

McLeod / Schell Case Solution Form 1

McLeod / Schell Case Solution Form 2
Elements of the Firm as a System

Case: **Council of 100**   Name: _____

Objectives and/or Standards:

Output:

Management and Organization:

Information Processor:

Inputs and Input Resources:

Transformation Process:

Output Resources:

McLeod / Schell Case Solution Form 3
Subsystems of the Firm

Case: <u>Council of 100</u>　　　　　　　　**Name:** _____

Subsystem:

Subsystem:

Subsystem:

Subsystem:

McLeod / Schell Case Solution Form 4
Problems and Symptoms

Case: <u>Council of 100</u>   Name: _____

Environment:
Objectives and/or Standards:
Output:
Management and Organization:
Information Processor:
Inputs and Physical System:

Main Problem(s):

1.

2.

3.

McLeod / Schell Case Solution Form 5
Alternatives

Case: **Council of 100**　　　　　　　　Name: _____

Alternative:

　Advantages:

　Disadvantages:

Alternative:

　Advantages:

　Disadvantages:

McLeod / Schell Case Solution Form 5
Alternatives

Case: **Council of 100**   Name: _____

Alternative:

  Advantages:

  Disadvantages:

Alternative:

  Advantages:

  Disadvantages:

McLeod / Schell Case Solution Form 6
Decision and Implementation

Case: <u>Council of 100</u>   **Name:** _____

Decision:

Implementation Resources Needed:

Implementation Steps to be Followed:

UNIVERSITY COMPUTING

The university has been trying to deal with electronic communications issues for some time. Like most universities, the number of students, staff, and faculty using computer resources to send electronic mail (e-mail) and other computer mediated communications had exploded during the last ten years. A computing advisory statement was approved by the faculty senate and signed by the administration last year, but the document was quite out of date as soon as it was signed. There are not any specific guidelines and nobody is sure that a list of allowed and disallowed actions is appropriate. A specific set of actions would always be out of date because new possibilities in electronic communications are always being found.

At the same time that use of computer resources has skyrocketed, threats from computer viruses have increased in frequency and in menace. Viruses that posted messages such as "Have A Nice Day" gave way to viruses that destroyed all data on the computer. E-mail communications were frequently used to send these damaging viruses to many people who did not understand the danger of accepting computer programs from unknown sources. The policy for using computer resources would have to address both the frivolous use of computer resources, as well as the threats from viruses. Someone that received a virus and passed it to other university users, by accident or by intent, could cause the university a great deal of damage.

Jeff Lamb is the associate director of Computing Services and it is his responsibility to help the university determine its policy for using computer resources. Once the university's policy is determined, he has the responsibility to enforce the policy. Students who violate the policy are dealt with by the Dean of Students. Faculty and staff are referred to the Human Resources Division. Jeff has formed a committee to help develop a section on computer resource use for the university's computing advisory statement. The statement will be accepted, amended, or rejected by the university, but the university relies heavily upon committees to form policy.

Jeff will chair the committee whose members have been chosen so that all segments of the university are represented. The committee will be fairly large once it officially meets, about 35 members. Jeff has appointed a small steering committee that will help decide the agenda for the committee when it begins meeting. Of course, any committee member will still be able to bring other concerns before the entire committee. Jeff wants the preliminary meeting by the steering committee to be a brainstorming session to bring a wide variety of ideas out into the open.

The steering committee members (besides Jeff) are:

Bob Harnett - Business School Professor
Susan O'Neal - Associate Dean of Students
Len Charnes - Student Computer Consultant

Each member brings a different prospective to the committee. Bob Harnett uses electronic communications extensively in the classes he teaches. All students turn in his assignments via e-mail. There are short projects in each class that deal with finding resources on the Internet. Bob has used electronic communications extensively and is familiar with most of the problems the students encounter.

Bob has students download free software via the Internet. When students do this they learn about other sites for software. Sometimes the site is well known, such as AOL or Qualcomm or Microsoft. Often the site is a personal web page maintained by someone the student has never heard of before. So far, no programs downloaded by any of Bob's students has contained a virus.

Susan O'Neal did not use e-mail until last year when she began work at the university. The university where she had previously worked did not promote electronic communications since the computing director there felt e-mail and other applications would use too many computer resources. Susan is no longer a novice, but she still has a great deal to learn about electronic communications. Like many people, she knows several tricks and techniques and feels as though she is quite proficient. She has not yet realized that there is so much to learn about electronic communications that most people just learn enough to do their daily tasks.

Len Charnes is beginning the fall semester of his senior year. He worked in the computer lab as a consultant last year and quickly became one of the people that students and faculty turned to when they had a difficult problem to solve. He has an intuitive understanding of the software used in the labs. Len's perspective is strictly that of a user. He has never had to deal with trying to ensure security or rationing the few computer resources among all of the students, staff, and faculty that need them. His philosophy is simple: let people use computers as much as they can with as little interference as possible by the administrators of the university.

Jeff didn't choose the members of the steering committee to solve problems and then bring a set of answers to the entire committee to be voted upon. The steering committee is charged with brainstorming issues and trying to explain the pros and cons of each issue. To that end, the steering committee must have a diverse set of opinions and expertise. Computer mediated communication promises to be a difficult and controversial subject for the university.

Viruses will be even more difficult because the university does not have the resources to restore files and software to all faculty and staff in the event that a destructive virus strikes even 10% of the university's microcomputers. The disruption to classes and university functions would be a terrible blow. A serious virus attack, if unchecked, could effectively shut the university down for a week or longer.

Jeff Lamb: I'm glad to see each of you today. I'd like this first meeting of the steering committee to be one where we all feel comfortable and secure enough to bring up any concerns we might have. I have no intention of penalizing anyone who has opinions different from mine or different from the university's stated policies. In fact, we need to carefully look at current policies and determine if they meet our needs. Computer mediated communications have exploded recently, certainly faster than the guidelines we use to control them.

E-mail has been the fastest growing part of our computing profile, but the total amount of resources used for it are still a relatively small part of the overall budget. Major issues really concern how we use it.

Also, we've been assailed by computer virus attacks more than twelve times during the last academic year. We were lucky. The first time it happened, the virus was sent to a systems programmer at the university's operating center. The programmer called the webmaster and had the e-mail server shut down immediately. Then the virus was isolated, erased, and a "patch" to the virus protection software on the e-mail server was installed so that the virus could not infect any other computer resources on the campus. Since then we've kept the e-mail server up-to-date with virus checking software. Old viruses can be caught, but of course it doesn't catch new viruses.

Jeff then introduced each member of the steering committee. The members took about five minutes each to tell a little bit about their background. The time was spent getting to know one another and finding out phone numbers and e-mail addresses. The atmosphere was casual and the members of the steering committee soon felt comfortable with each other.

Jeff Lamb: I don't want to discuss any important issues today. I'd like for each of you to make a list of concerns you have about computer mediated communications and bring it to our next meeting which will be on Wednesday the 15th. Pay particular interest to e-mail. That's the area where most controversy has occurred during the last two years.

Now that electronic communications are a full section of the computer literacy course for all freshmen, we've seen a large increase in inappropriate use of e-mail. [Len interrupts.]

Len Charnes: That's not a fair statement. There's a big difference between what two people might think of as "inappropriate." Doug (a staff member who works for Jeff) tried to get a student's account canceled last semester because the student used e-mail to ask her friends about getting a ride to an out-of-town concert.

Isn't e-mail *supposed* to be used so that students get very familiar with using it in everyday stuff? Don't students *pay* technology fees that cover computer access?

Jeff Lamb: I know the incident you're talking about. Doug misunderstood what the student was trying to do. And it was made more confusing when the "friends" you are talking about turned out to be over 350 students, the whole list of students taking the computer literacy course that semester.

We need to look at the most common ways that people on this campus use e-mail and we need to understand what guidelines will help all of us be more secure in their use.

Bob Harnett: I'm not sure I'm comfortable with making guidelines that end up being a list of rules that restrict computer use. What I think you're saying, Jeff, is that rules and/or guidelines will be made by the whole committee. Our job as a steering committee is to make sure all of the issues that bear upon making good guidelines are explored by the committee. A variety of viewpoints need to be presented for each issue.

Jeff Lamb: Actually, the recommendations of our committee go to a university committee with authority to implement our suggestions. But you're right, our job as a steering committee is to brainstorm the issues to be placed before our whole committee. And that could mean that you have to argue both sides of any given issue, even the side that you don't think should prevail.

I don't think Len feels any restrictions on e-mail use are required. But I believe that he could make a fair list of issues that could be argued in favor of some restrictions. Each of you has a perspective that needs to be brought to the committee. We are a diverse campus, we need diverse points of view in order to accommodate the whole campus community. And I really mean "community."

One severe problem is the spread of computer viruses on the campus. I'd like e-mail and viruses considered as related issues. These viruses frequently come attached to e-mail. When e-mail messages with viruses are opened they can do terrible things to the computer. Files can be damaged or erased. Students that lose semester projects may get failing grades or have to retake courses.

Len Charnes: That's not fair. It isn't the student's fault that the computer got a virus. The professor should give them a grade and not count the project.

Bob Harnett: That's not going to happen. No project, no grade. Students cannot use the e-mail equivalent of "the dog ate my homework" because it's the student's responsibility to keep a safe copy somewhere even if that means a paper copy stored in a desk drawer.

Susan O'Neal: Can we talk to other people as we make up our list of issues?

Jeff Lamb: Yes. Try to be as open as possible to the concerns that faculty, staff, and students have. Don't forget that about 5% of our students are foreign nationals. They come here with a wide variety of education and cultural backgrounds. They're part of the community.

Susan O'Neal: And non-traditional students. 20% of our undergraduate students are over 22 years old. We see a number of students that went to work out of high school and have come back to get a college degree. A lot of them have e-mail accounts from AOL or other Internet service providers. Many automatically forward e-mail from their school accounts to their personal accounts or vice versa.

Bob Harnett: Many of them had staff jobs, then, when the economy slowed down, they were laid off as companies reorganized. But they certainly have computer skills. They may not have been taught why they were using technology or what the big picture might be but they do know how to use technology for their job tasks.

That seems to be a big problem. Knowing how to do something but not understanding why or how it is done is dangerous. It's like taking a chain saw to cut down a pole because you know how to use a chain saw. Not understanding that the pole supports a high voltage electrical wire can cause major problems. We've got a lot of people with just enough e-mail knowledge to be dangerous.

E-mail isn't a sophisticated application of technology but it can be a good predictor of how much information technology a person has assimilated into his or her job. To get the full potential of e-mail you have to know about the computer system in your organization, file manipulation, some communications concepts, and more.

The same can be said for virus knowledge. These non-traditional students come from an environment where the company provided sophisticated software and a large support staff to actively seek out and prevent virus damage. We don't have that luxury at a college. We've got to make them understand that they have to know what to look for and not expect us to clean up their mess.

Jeff Lamb: Okay, I think we know where we want to go now. Bring your list of issues to the next meeting with the pros and cons for each issue. Be prepared to argue all sides of the issues. Don't be afraid to bring up an issue that you think would be controversial or silly. Unless we deal with the issues here, it's unlikely that we can set guidelines for university computer mediated communications. I'll see you on the 15th.

The steering committee members worked on their lists during the time before the next meeting. Len asked a number of other student computer consultants about their experiences. He thought that they would all share his opinion; that no restrictions should be made on electronic communications. Instead he found that the student computer consultant opinions included everything from limiting the amount of time students were allowed to use e-mail to letting the general public have complete access since the university was funded with tax dollars. What further surprised Len was that each student consultant was adamant that she or he was right.

Bob Harnett turned to his classes to help him gather information. Each student was to make a list of good and bad things about their access to e-mail. He collected all of the responses and categorized them. Next he asked other faculty about using electronic communications. Most of the faculty used them frequently, but mainly as electronic note passing. Only about 10% of their use would be considered sophisticated.

Bob sent a second survey to his students concerning computer viruses. It asked if the students understood what computer viruses were, how they spread, if the student had antivirus software on his or her computer, and if the student's computer had ever been infected by a virus.

Susan O'Neal made her own list and then asked some of her colleagues to comment on it. She didn't find many that had strong opinions about electronic communications issues. Most felt comfortable with what they were using. They looked at electronic mail as the only application they needed to understand and they didn't really care to know any fancy features, only the basics.

Viruses were somebody else's problem. Like the non-traditional students, Susan found that staff felt the university should keep viruses from them. It was almost like citizens in a community that expected the police to show up at their door the moment trouble started but who didn't believe citizens themselves had any responsibility for law and order.

The only exception was a graduate student (Nancy) who worked part-time in Susan's office. Nancy's home computer had become infected with a virus from an e-mail attachment. The virus destroyed several files on her computer before Nancy was able to "clean" the disk and get rid of the virus. One of the destroyed files was a semester-long project that Nancy was almost ready to turn in to her professor. Luckily, the professor still had a copy of a rough draft that had been turned in on paper earlier. Nancy rewrote the paper from the draft, but she missed the deadline for the project by two days. The professor deducted one letter grade from the project because it was turned in late. Susan began to feel that there were more issues to computer resource use than she knew existed.

Everyone was well prepared for the next steering committee meeting. Jeff had several very large sheets of paper taped onto the walls so the group could map out ideas as it brainstormed the issues. He had different colored markers so different ideas could be highlighted.

Jeff Lamb: I see each of you has brought a list, that's very good. I think the first thing we want to do is begin by making a list of issues we think are important. I'll put that list on this middle sheet of paper. Then we'll put the advantages on the right side and the disadvantages on the left.

Susan O'Neal: I think that before we list advantages and disadvantages we need to really understand the list of issues. I thought I understood the issues before I started talking to some of the people in my office, but now I'm not so sure. And if I don't understand the subject, I don't know if I should be an authority on deciding what the issues should be.

Jeff Lamb: That's a good point. Maybe we can just try to reach some consensus on the issues. Then we can start looking into the pros and cons later, maybe at another meeting if we run out of time today.

Susan, why don't you begin. Give me a couple of issues you think are important and then I'll go around the room until everybody has given all the issues that he or she feels are important. Then we'll try to state the issues in generic terms so that they apply to the entire campus community.

Susan O'Neal: Okay. The first issue I have is restriction from information access. The second is a need to provide all users with a good understanding of all relevant features of electronic communications.

Bob Harnett: My first issue is longer hours for the computer labs. The second is e-mail privacy.

Len Charnes: My issues are lack of privacy and the inability to find out the username of people so that we can send messages to classmates.

Jeff Lamb: Let's stop here for a minute and take a look at what we have. Len, I'm not quite sure that your two issues are compatible. Explain what you mean by privacy.

Len Charnes: Lots of students do homework in the labs. Their teachers require them to type their reports so they use a word processing package in the computer labs. There are lots of examples where one student might think another can read his notes as they are being typed into the word processor so doing homework in the computer lab is like taking a risk that someone else will copy your homework.

But the biggest complaints are about the embarrassment report and the conflict exercise.

Susan O'Neal: I don't know what those are.

Len Charnes: The embarrassment report is for the psychology class that everyone has to take as a required course. It's due about the third week of every semester. By that time the computer labs are packed; every machine is being used and there is usually someone waiting behind you for their turn on the computer.

So you have your notes about the most embarrassing thing that's happened to you during the last year and anybody sitting next to you or standing behind you can read your notes.

We get people all of the time that get stuck and need help but they don't want you to look at the screen because they don't want you to know what embarrassed them. You can't help them if you can't see the screen.

The conflict exercise is from the management class. They have a section in the text that deals with managing personal conflicts and the professor has students describe conflict that a student has had with a friend and explain how the conflict was resolved. Then the students are supposed to predict how the conflict could have been settled or avoided if they had applied the principles learned in the course.

Jeff Lamb: That explains the privacy issue but what about finding out classmates' usernames?

Bob Harnett: I think Len means that many classes have students work in groups. Since class schedules conflict and because some students live pretty far from campus, groups are beginning to meet using e-mail instead of meeting face-to-face. If you know someone's name you still don't know the username because the university assigns usernames in code.

Jeff Lamb: That's not true. Anyone can access the student phone book from a terminal. The username will be in the phone book.

Bob Harnett: Not quite. The total quality team working on the phone book project found that almost 80% of the students in the phone book had missing or incorrect phone numbers and e-mail addresses. The problem is timing, student phone books need to be delivered to students as soon as possible during the semester. But many students don't know their usernames before the semester starts. So they can't fill out that information when they complete the forms for phone book information.

Jeff Lamb: I see what you mean. "Access" doesn't mean that something is possible, it has to mean that people who want to use the service can do so with a reasonable amount of effort.

Susan O'Neal: This is part of the issue of information access I brought up. What responsibility does the computer group have to educate faculty, staff, and students about the e-mail features? And what about viruses?

Jeff Lamb: That's a difficult question to answer. The responsibility of the university to its students and workers concerns how one person's use of computer resources can prevent another person from access, and a host of other considerations. Let's get back to the list for now.

Len Charnes: It seems that as we talk, the list of issues becomes smaller but more general. When we started today we were going to give pros and cons on issues, but we decided to just make a list of issues instead. Now I can make an argument that only two issues should be on the list; access and security. But maybe they are two sides of the same coin.

Susan O'Neal: A graduate student in my office says that she lost files from her computer because a virus from an e-mail attachment infected her files. Jeff, do you know what she's talking about?

Jeff Lamb: We field a number of questions from students about viruses. But the university's policy is that students are responsible for installing antivirus software on their computers; the university has no role in that regard.

Len Charnes: Don't you mean the administration would like to avoid the cost of antivirus software?

Jeff Lamb: No, the university has a site license for antivirus software that all university employees may install on their computers at work.

Len Charnes: That doesn't make sense. A lot of students and staff do work on their computers at home and if they get an infected file there, they can bring it to the computers on campus. The policy about loading antivirus software is ineffective unless it covers **all** the computers where campus related work is conducted.

Susan O'Neal: I hate to show my ignorance, but what exactly is antivirus software?

Jeff Lamb: Companies like Symantec make antivirus software. They can be found at http://symantec.com on the Internet. The Norton antivirus software packages are sold by Symantec. McAfee Corporation (at mcafee.com) is another common software package. The reason why so many people know about them is that many computer manufacturers include basic antivirus software as part of the package coming with a new computer.
    Then you can buy the full package if you want. Most antivirus software vendors have websites so that you can download the most recent files for virus detection. That way the package stays current even as new viruses are developed.

Susan O'Neal: I had no idea all of this was available from our computer system here on campus. And I feel a little cheated that nobody from Computing Services has told me about them.

Len Charnes: But we need to look at the issue of ethics. Is it ethical for the people in Computing Services to know about all of these services, to know they'd benefit the rest of the university, and to simply not tell us that they are available?

Jeff Lamb: That's a loaded question. I could easily ask if it's ethical that students don't take responsibility for finding out what is available. Faculty and staff would know if they check our web page; we have a link to the security page followed by the link to antivirus information. Then just fill out a two page questionnaire and we'll give you access to the antivirus software within two weeks.
    We don't hide many services. The services are there and we are willing to help if students and faculty are willing to ask. It shouldn't be our responsibility to tell everybody every possible feature available to them. Computer users have the responsibility to look for themselves.

Bob Harnett: Both sides of that question are arguable. But I feel the Computing Services people are responsible to let the computing community on campus know of software that is critical. I mean, if we ever got seriously hit by a damaging virus we could lose so many computer files that we might have to close the university for a semester. We've got alternate computing plans for hurricanes, tornadoes, and fire, but viruses seem to be just as dangerous, if not more dangerous. And Computing Services makes sure the hurricane, tornado, and fire plans are widely distributed to every university worker.
    Also, the professor who makes an assignment about an embarrassing incident knowing that the student will have to risk exposure in order to type up the assignment bothers me. Professors don't make students reveal such information in an open classroom because of the embarrassment it could cause. We have some real issues about access and privacy and viruses. I don't think we have enough time to sort them all out today.

Jeff Lamb: I agree. It seems that this steering committee is regressing to more and more fundamental issues. I'd like for each of you to write a paragraph or a page about access and privacy and another page about computer viruses. We need to meet in about two weeks to see where we stand. I'd still like for us to be able to bring something to the whole committee so that guidelines for electronic mediated communications can be determined. These e-mails are more than just content because of assignments that are sent via e-mail and viruses can be spread by e-mail. The only thing I'm sure of is that the problems will become more difficult as time goes on.

QUESTIONS:

1. Contact your university computing services department and find out what antivirus precautions are available to you as a student of the university. Find an Internet site of a company that sells antivirus software and describe the features of the software.

2. The "embarrassment report" is an example that raises ethical issues. Is the professor that made an assignment that potentially embarrasses students using sound ethical judgment? You might visit the Association for Computing Machinery's web site at http://www.acm.org/constitution/code.html to view their code of ethics.

3. The Computing Services Department in the case might argue that they provide access to the software required by faculty and staff but Susan O'Neal feels cheated. What responsibility does the Computing Services Department have to let university faculty, students, and staff know the full potential of computing resources? Should they at least publicize information that is likely to be desired by a large portion of faculty, staff, and students?

4. Assume that you are an employer and you provide your employees with access to the Internet. What do you believe are reasonable steps your information systems group should take to keep viruses from computers?

McLeod / Schell Case Solution Form 1
The Problem Setting

Case: <u>University Computing</u>   **Name:** _____

Environmental Elements:

Important Facts:

McLeod / Schell Case Solution Form 2
Elements of the Firm as a System

Case: <u>University Computing</u>　　　　　　**Name:** _____

Objectives and/or Standards:

Output:

Management and Organization:

Information Processor:

Inputs and Input Resources:

Transformation Process:

Output Resources:

McLeod / Schell Case Solution Form 3
Subsystems of the Firm

Case: <u>University Computing</u>   **Name:** _____

Subsystem:

Subsystem:

Subsystem:

Subsystem:

McLeod / Schell Case Solution Form 4
Problems and Symptoms

Case: <u>University Computing</u>　　　　　　　　**Name:** _____

Environment:
Objectives and/or Standards:
Output:
Management and Organization:
Information Processor:
Inputs and Physical System:

Main Problem(s):

1.

2.

3.

McLeod / Schell Case Solution Form 5
Alternatives

Case: <u>University Computing</u>   **Name:** _____

Alternative:

  Advantages:

  Disadvantages:

Alternative:

  Advantages:

  Disadvantages:

McLeod / Schell Case Solution Form 5
Alternatives

Case: University Computing			**Name:** _____

Alternative:

   Advantages:

   Disadvantages:

Alternative:

   Advantages:

   Disadvantages:

McLeod / Schell Case Solution Form 6
Decision and Implementation

Case: University Computing   **Name:** _____

Decision:

Implementation Resources Needed:

Implementation Steps to be Followed:

ECOLOGIX TECHNOLOGIES

Ecologix Technologies is a conglomerate consisting of nine subsidiary companies. All of the companies' operations are scattered throughout Australia. The subsidiaries are:

<u>Subsidiary Company</u>

A discount drug chain (20 stores)
An oil and gas exploration company
A food processing and distribution company
A manufacturer of small hardware items
A store fixture manufacturing company
A money order company
A paper products manufacturer
A restaurant chain (8 restaurants)
A retail supermarket and convenience store chain (more than 300 stores)

The store fixture company produces store fixtures for the supermarkets, convenience stores, restaurants, and drug stores. The money orders are sold in the various retail outlets. A number of the items sold in the supermarkets and convenience stores are produced and delivered by the food processing company, and so on. With the exception of the oil and gas company, the firms fit together to form an efficient distribution network.

Most of the computing is performed at the conglomerate headquarters in Melbourne. Transaction data is gathered at each company location and transmitted to the subsidiary headquarters and then to the Melbourne data center where it is processed. The reports are distributed to managers in the conglomerate headquarters and to the various company headquarters by intranet (i.e. Internet-like format but only available to Ecologix employees). Ecologix believes in highly centralized computer use.

Ecologix began operations as the Levinson Company, a food processing and distribution operation that was founded in the 1940s by Kalman A. Levinson. Kalman, or Kal as he was called, started with a single grain elevator at a railway siding on the plains of New South Wales. These elevators were expanded into fourteen food warehouses located throughout New South Wales. An aggressive sales force, working out of the warehouses, did such a good job of selling their products to food retailers that the Levinson brand became one of the most popular in the country. To people in the food industry, "Kal's Company" was one of the best.

Kal Levinson died in 1979 and left the bulk of his estate to his brother Myron. Myron was getting along in years and had no interest in shouldering the responsibilities of the expanding organization, so he gave half of his stock to his son, Gregg, and split the remainder among his other heirs.

After earning a bachelors degree in econometrics and business statistics from the University of Sydney, Gregg Levinson had made a name for himself working his way up the ranks to become the president of a Northern Territory supermarket chain. He transformed the chain from a few run-down stores into an expanding, profitable, and efficient retailing system. Shortly after assuming the presidency of the Levinson Company, Gregg acquired a controlling interest in the stock of his former supermarket chain and brought it under the umbrella of the Levinson operations. This proved to be a wise move and sparked the chain of acquisitions that eventually led to the Ecologix conglomerate.

One of Gregg's first actions when he took over Levinson was to hire his old college roommate, Jay Schreuter, as his executive vice president. During the time that Gregg had been transforming the Northern Territory supermarket chain, Jay had been achieving similar success as a vice president for an Adelaide bank. With Jay on board, the two set out to develop an improved organization structure to guide the expanding operations. It became Jay's responsibility to find competent people to fill each slot in the organization either with existing employees or with new hires. In some cases, existing managers were retained, in others, new people were brought on board.

In his banking job, Jay had become close friends with Glenn Richards, the associate director of the management information systems department for one of the bank's largest commercial customers--a manufacturer of farm equipment. One day over lunch, Jay offered Richards the job of director of information services at Ecologix. At first Richards insisted that his title be vice president, but Jay explained that the computer had played a relatively minor role in Ecologix in the past and that Gregg did not believe that the operation currently warranted a vice president. Jay also said that Gregg was oriented primarily toward merchandising and financial matters and regarded the computer operation as a support function. Although Richards wasn't impressed with the status of information services at

Ecologix, he was confident that he could turn things around and he decided to accept the challenge. Richards accepted Jay's job offer and said that he was looking forward to finally getting a chance to "run the whole IS show."

The previous director of information services, Johnnie Vinson, had voluntarily stepped down to assume leadership of the systems development group. Information services is divided into three main groups--systems development, systems support, and computer operations. Johnnie loved systems development and had never really been happy managing the entire department. Johnnie was well liked by the other members of the department and they laughed when Richards jokingly announced to the assembled staff that Johnnie would now be able to "catch up on her loafing."

Richards immediately made his presence known by hiring a new systems support manager and convincing Jay that more computing equipment and personnel were needed. An additional mainframe computer was acquired to increase the processing capacity by 60 percent, and the number of people in the department doubled.

Even with the new hardware and expanded staff, information services had a hard time keeping up with the increasing demands caused by the successes of each of the Ecologix companies. The data entry section worked a regular 40-hour week, but the rest of the computer staff was on call around the clock and some of the critical personnel logged as many as twenty overtime hours a week.

Many of the staff worried that they might not be able to hold up under such pressure and wondered just how long the present resources would be adequate. Such pessimism was never expressed by Richards or other higher level managers, however, who exuded a confidence that everything was going as planned.

Jay was content with Richards and felt that the computer operation was in good hands. Jay then turned his attention to another area that he also considered important--the accounting department. Ecologix could not be well managed unless the accounting systems of the subsidiaries worked together. When Jay joined Ecologix, neither the accounting director nor the managers of the five sections (accounts receivable, accounts payable, payroll, store accounting, and general accounting) had college degrees in accounting. The more Jay learned about the situation, the more concerned he became. One day a clerk in the store accounting section casually mentioned that "These books have never balanced. At the end of the month, Kal would add whatever was necessary to balance out. He'd usually adjust it from an account that nobody knew much about, like depreciation or fixed assets."

Jay decided that a house cleaning was in order, so he started at the top by hiring a new chief financial officer, Doris Hill. Hill was lured from her job as a partner of a Melbourne auditing firm. Although many candidates had responded to the job advertisement, Hill stood out as a person who could get the job done. When Jay was telling Gregg about his new hire he said, "She's really going to get in there and crack some heads."

Hill did exactly that. She reorganized the departmental structure into seven sections: store accounting, retail operations, warehousing operations, accounts receivable, accounts payable, purchasing, and banking and finance. All of the old section heads retained their management positions but were given the assignment of taking courses in accounting and management at a local two-year college. New section heads were brought in for the purchasing and the banking and finance sections, and both had accounting degrees.

In addition to strengthening the management team within the accounting department, Hill was instrumental in communicating a strong departmental image to the other Ecologix units. The position of chief financial officer was one of considerable power, and Hill didn't hesitate to use it. As an example, prior to Hill, the store managers had taken their time in submitting their weekly sales reports. It was not unusual for the reports to arrive in Melbourne five days after the cutoff date. Hill simply advised the managers that if she didn't get the reports on time she would put them down for zero sales that week and see what Jay would do about that.

The changes that Gregg and Jay made in the original organization paid off. The parent company continued to grow and prosper and the carefully orchestrated additions of the various subsidiary companies produced an efficient, vertically integrated operation aimed at satisfying consumer food and drug needs. What used to be called "Kal's Company" was now "Gregg and Jay's Company."

One afternoon, after the problems of the day had been solved, the two were reflecting on their accomplishments. All of the talk had been positive until Gregg startled Jay by saying, "You know, I think we might have a problem somewhere in the organization. We're losing too many good people. I've noticed that our turnover rate is especially high in accounting and information services. We hire people, train them, and about the time they become productive, they leave to work somewhere else, very often for our competitors. Any ideas Jay?"

"I've seen those figures, Gregg," Jay replied. "But I don't think we're any worse off than other companies. Those are two areas where the competition is fierce. There aren't enough good accountants and computer people to go around. The computer people especially take advantage of it. They know they can get a 10 percent increase in salary simply by going to work for another company. I don't think we should play that game. We should keep salaries low, let them move on when they're ready, and bring in replacements at the entry-level salaries. That's a good way to keep costs down."

Jay's explanation seemed to satisfy Gregg that the turnover problem wasn't serious, but several months later they had another problem on their hands. Gregg called Jay into his office and as Jay walked in he saw that Gregg was reading a letter. Gregg had a determined look on his face as he read to Jay--"Very inaccurate. Incorrect application of policies. Serious misstatement of actual holdings." Gregg looked up and said "Jay, do you know what I'm describing?"

Before Jay could respond, Gregg answered his own question. "It's our accounting system. This is what our auditing firm says about our accounting system. This is stronger language than they used when they were here last year. You assured me that you'd take care of it. It looks to me like you've dropped the ball. What's the story, Jay?"

During the next few days Gregg thought some more about the accounting problem and Jay's request that a reengineering project be initiated. Gregg decided to pursue the issue further and told Jay to assemble a review committee, composed of key people who could decide what to do and how to go about doing it. Gregg gave Jay six weeks to form the committee and come up with a solution.

Jay met with Richards and Hill, explained Gregg's directives, and told them that he expected them to serve. They both quickly accepted. Jay asked Richards to be the chairperson, and asked both Richards and Hill to recommend other committee members. Richards suggested that Johnnie Vinson join the group, and Hill recommended Bob Cornish, a member of the accounting department who knew the accounting systems of the subsidiaries and computer systems. All agreed that this group of five, including Jay, would be a good combination of accounting, computer, and management expertise to tackle the problem.

Richards, as chair of the committee, assembled the group together for its first meeting. He was prepared for long discussions about the accounting systems of the subsidiaries.

Jay Schreuter: Thanks for agreeing to serve on this committee. I know that it may take most of our time to simply get a handle on the accounting systems at each of the subsidiaries, but we only have six weeks. We've got to push through.

Glenn Richards: Doris and I have spent most of our effort in organizational issues since we took charge of the information systems and accounting groups. But we're at a point now where we need to dig deeper into the actual workings of the departments. I know I've left the managerial details of the systems development people to Johnnie because I believe those details are better handled by a manager close to the source of the work.

Now we have a problem that our auditors want us to fix. The accounting systems seem to have a flaw that creates inaccurate information. We obviously need to correct this problem.

Doris Hill: I've seen the auditors' report, but I guess I have a different perspective about what caused the problem. Ecologix has installed the same accounting information system software into each of the subsidiaries. The process was completed in late 1999 in order to make sure we didn't have a Y2K problem where the rollover of a two digit year field would make our programs think it was 1900 instead of 2000.

We had to fix that problem first, get all subsidiaries using the same vendor of a standardized accounting information system. Software was in place by the end of 1999 and we spent six months of 2000 fine tuning the software. Our problems are operational, not due to the information system itself.

Bob Cornish: Let me see if I can make some of the operational problems a little clearer. The operations, like a drilling operation for the oil and gas subsidiary, is supposed to be in touch with its subsidiary headquarters. The headquarters of each subsidiary is connected to the conglomerate headquarters via a secure communications line. We have what are called "leased lines," a private communications line connection that is secure and fast.

The trouble is that all accounting information has to be funneled to the subsidiary headquarters before it is sent down the secure communications line to us at conglomerate headquarters.

Johnnie Vinson: Why does all the accounting information have to travel from subsidiary headquarters to us? Why can't it come directly to our conglomerate headquarters in Melbourne?

Doris Hill: The information is sensitive, we have to assure that data security is maintained. Also, it has to be aggregated and sorted in the right order for our use.

Jay Schreuter: Let me get this straight, the problem is not the accounting software at all but it's a problem of getting the data to headquarters?

Bob Cornish: That's right. About that last auditors' report, they knew the figures were wrong, but they wrote the report anyway.

Jay Schreuter: I don't understand.

Doris Hill: The auditors scheduled two days to verify data here in Melbourne, a Tuesday and Wednesday. Well, the drilling operation 30 miles off Perth was in the middle of a bad storm. They were transmitting their data when their power went out. It was out for two days.
    Now the data that was transmitted said that twenty barrels of crude had been produced the week before. Everybody knew it was a mistake. But the auditors wrote down twenty. When the drilling operation restored power on Thursday they resent their production data; twenty *thousand* barrels of crude were produced.
    By then the auditors were gone and they noted we misstated our assets. The reason was that we were using that week's crude oil production as part of the collateral for a loan to start another well. Everyone knew the originally transmitted data was a mistake but the auditors took it at face value saying it was "the conservative thing to do." It wasn't a problem for the bank, they went ahead with the loan.

Johnnie Vinson: I don't understand why we allow a bottleneck of data flow to occur between the subsidiary headquarters and Melbourne. Don't you remember the heat wave of 1998? The city electricity generators went down and caused a major power station fire. The power station was next to the main telephone exchange station for Melbourne and it burned too. That put the city on 20% of normal communications volume for two weeks. We could hardly get data from the subsidiaries. Communications volume was rationed to critical areas of medical facilities and public utilities first and businesses last.
    At that time we all complained because our accounting information systems represent almost 80% of our computing resource usage and we couldn't get the data we needed to run the applications. Didn't we learn anything from the 1998 experience?

Jay Schreuter: Johnnie has a point. Doris, you won't allow weekly sales reports to come in late from store managers, so there is no reason to accept reports late from the subsidiaries.

Doris Hill: That means the subsidiaries won't be doing the aggregation and assimilation of data before passing it to us at conglomerate headquarters. And they won't be using leased lines so communications won't be secure. That's a real threat to our sensitive corporate information.

Johnnie Vinson: But the Internet connections can be as secure as a leased line. There are virtual private networks. They work as securely as a leased line but can be established between any two points on the Internet for the few seconds it takes to send the data securely.
    If it's good enough for credit card companies it should be good enough for us. Anyway, the transactions from the operations to the subsidiary headquarters are not over secure lines. If you put those transmissions on a virtual private network we'd be more secure than we are now.

    At this point Jay Schreuter took over the meeting again. He explained that the discussion had caught him by surprise, he thought the problem was accounting software. Now he realized that it was something else entirely. He told the group that three separate vendors had contacted Ecologix about their computer and accounting operations. He had been interested in their views because his focus centered on organizational structure and staffing. Now he would consider their preliminary proposals.
    IBM, Perot Systems, and Andersen Consulting offered three similar proposals. The crux of each was the use of an intranet to move data around the company instead of the funneling of data through subsidiary headquarters. It would be as secure as the current leased line system, it would be cheaper, and it would avoid the bottleneck of data

flow through subsidiary headquarters. If all three recommended the same general plan, then Jay felt there must be a good reason for using an intranet for data transfer.

Jay asked the committee members not to discuss the proposals. He had always focused on organizational structure and staffing and this would decrease morale if it was not handled properly. Jay assured everyone that there would be no immediate decision and that any decision would be made only after the issues were discussed openly with the affected areas of accounting and information systems. The proposals would have been discussed sooner but Jay had thought the accounting information systems problem was more pressing. Now he believed that accounting information systems, per se, were not the problem.

The committee members were unprepared for the news. Doris Hill was particularly surprised since such conversations were being held without her knowledge and she was the chief financial officer. Glenn Richards wondered what the impact would be to his people. Would a new group be added? Or would information systems be outsourced to IBM or one of the other vendors?

QUESTIONS:

1. List advantages and disadvantages of using a virtual private network as opposed to leased lines for communication.

2. What role did Gregg Levinson and Jay Schreuter play in the misunderstanding that accounting information system software was the cause of the problem?

3. Two basic management skills are communication and decision making. Give several examples at Ecologix where each of these areas are inadequate.

4. Ecologix might be about to experience high employee turnover. Jay Schreuter prides himself on his organizational structure and staffing abilities, what can he do to prevent or lessen high turnover?

5. Use your text or an Internet site to learn more about intranets. How will the speed of data flow change and will data flow from subsidiaries to the conglomerate be more or less centralized if an intranet is used?

6. Was Richards the right person to serve as chair of the committee? Who do you believe was the 'real' chair as opposed to merely the person with the title?

7. What role or roles would you assign to Doris Hill and Glenn Richards as discussions with IBM, Perot Systems, and Andersen Consulting move forward?

8. How would you rate Gregg Levinson and Jay Schreuter as managers and why?

McLeod / Schell Case Solution Form 1
The Problem Setting

Case: <u>Ecologix Technologies</u>   **Name:** _____

Environmental Elements:

Important Facts:

McLeod / Schell Case Solution Form 2
Elements of the Firm as a System

Case: **Ecologix Technologies** Name: _____

Objectives and/or Standards:
Output:
Management and Organization:
Information Processor:
Inputs and Input Resources:
Transformation Process:
Output Resources:

McLeod / Schell Case Solution Form 3
Subsystems of the Firm

Case: Ecologix Technologies   **Name:** _____

Subsystem:

Subsystem:

Subsystem:

Subsystem:

McLeod / Schell Case Solution Form 4
Problems and Symptoms

Case: <u>Ecologix Technologies</u>　　　　　　**Name:** _____

Environment:
Objectives and/or Standards:
Output:
Management and Organization:
Information Processor:
Inputs and Physical System:

Main Problem(s):

1.

2.

3.

67

McLeod / Schell Case Solution Form 5
Alternatives

Case: <u>Ecologix Technologies</u>　　　　　**Name:** _____

Alternative:

  Advantages:

  Disadvantages:

Alternative:

  Advantages:

  Disadvantages:

McLeod / Schell Case Solution Form 5
Alternatives

Case: <u>Ecologix Technologies</u>   **Name:** _____

Alternative:

  Advantages:

  Disadvantages:

Alternative:

  Advantages:

  Disadvantages:

McLeod / Schell Case Solution Form 6
Decision and Implementation

Case: Ecologix Technologies   **Name:** _____

Decision:

Implementation Resources Needed:

Implementation Steps to be Followed:

MIDWEST FARM SUPPLIES

Bob Deer has worked for Midwest Farm Supplies since he graduated from college. He started as an assistant manager in a distribution center that serviced 14 counties in Ohio. The title made the job sound prestigious, but much of the work was physical. He scheduled the trucks and shipments of products to customers located in his area. He also helped load the trucks.

The experience had been excellent. Bob knew the products that Midwest sold. He could tell you their price, capacities, shipping weights, expected life, and many other important facts. The best part was that he enjoyed his job. He felt that farming was the most important occupation in America and he felt he had an important part to play in keeping farmers supplied with the materials they needed.

Bob was promoted to the state director for Iowa when Midwest started operations there. He would manage the operations of the two distribution centers: Cherokee and Cedar Rapids. Since sales representatives were assigned to distribution centers, Bob was responsible for them as well.

The road to the state director job was built on years of accomplishments. Bob worked for Midwest for six years before he was promoted to manager of his distribution center. Three years after that he was promoted to the largest distribution center in Indiana. He had the reputation of solving difficult problems. He knew when to solve a problem by simply working harder, when to use traditional methods, and when imagination was needed.

Lucy Rollins was assigned to manage the Cherokee center and Will Kirk was assigned to Cedar Rapids. Lucy had been the assistant manager of a distribution center in Ohio. She had 22 years of sales experience; 14 selling tractors for the leading tractor manufacturer and 8 with Midwest. She was able to manage her time well and was very organized. It was unusual that an assistant manager would be promoted to manage a large, new distribution center. Lucy earned the promotion by the level of service she provided to the sales staff.

Will had 7 years of experience with Midwest as manager of a distribution center. He had spent almost 20 years of his professional life in the sales of seed and fertilizer. He worked in the distribution center of one of Midwest's competitors for three years before joining Midwest. Will understood the needs of sales reps and the needs of the farmers. He owned a farm while he sold seed and fertilizer, so he had experience as a farmer. He feels very comfortable in the Cedar Rapids center and manages a staff that is very productive.

Midwest Farm Supplies was founded as a department store for farmers. It provides tractors, rakes, hay balers, irrigation supplies, plows, harnesses, and hundreds of other items. Midwest began operations in 1931 and had distribution centers in Ohio, Indiana, and Illinois. The business was sound and had produced steady profits for 70 years.

Headquarters for Midwest are located in Akron, Ohio. Financial services, marketing, and other corporate functions are performed there. Product was not manufactured by Midwest, it was purchased from a supplier or it was manufactured for Midwest. For example, Midwest's tractors were built by one of the large construction vehicle manufacturers. The design and specifications were provided by Midwest. This allowed Midwest to develop its own specifications for tractors without having to operate the manufacturing plant.

Most of the products sold by Midwest were shipped by railroad cars to distribution centers. The weight of the products were such that rail freight costs were substantially cheaper than any other transportation mode. When an order was ready to be shipped to a customer, the distribution center assembled it into one "load" and placed it on a tractor trailer. One order could take an entire tractor trailer or more but a trailer generally carried two to four loads at a time.

Farmers placed orders in two ways; a farmer could call (or write or fax) a Midwest distribution center and place the order directly. Most orders were placed through a Midwest sales rep. About 20% of the orders were placed directly by the customers but over 90% of the sales revenues were generated from sales reps.

Customers felt comfortable to place direct orders for some materials (such as PVC pipe or metal fence posts), but they often had questions to ask about products. It was difficult to talk to someone over a phone about water runoff and drainage problems. They wanted the face-to-face dialogue that sales reps provided. The sales rep had to see the problem in person to really understand it. The sales reps hired by Midwest were required to have farming experience. When they talked to the customers they could relate to their needs.

The need for sales reps to call on customers presented a problem. Farms were large and spread over large areas. Midwest typically rented office space in towns around the area so that farmers could contact the sales reps. One or two sales reps were assigned to each office and each distribution center serviced about ten offices. The office was staffed with a secretary and the usual office equipment; microcomputers, phones, desks, photocopy machines, and such. These arrangements worked well for Midwest for seventy years, but changes were needed in order to provide acceptable service in Iowa.

Iowa is sparsely populated compared to Ohio. The distances between farms are greater, so sales reps have to travel farther to service customers. There are fewer towns where Midwest can locate sales offices, and farmers would have to travel farther to get to the sales offices. The large, open areas are good for farms but they present serious problems for servicing customers.

Midwest requires management reports from the centers to Akron on a routine basis. All management personnel are familiar with all of the technology that supports the reports. Each distribution center performs most of its computing using microcomputers. Data and messages are shared easily since two or three of the microcomputers in each center are connected to the mainframe in Akron using modems and phone lines. Some of the systems in Akron are accessible using the Internet. Midwest employees have usernames and passwords to allow access to reports and other information not available to the general public.

Midwest has an electronic mail (e-mail) system and everyone who works for Midwest is assigned a computer account. A person's username is their last name plus their first initial. Electronic communication is used heavily by Midwest employees. Most feel they couldn't live without e-mail.

Midwest has a comprehensive computer training class for all new employees. They spend two weeks at Akron learning about the reports and applications available from headquarters. Next they learn about applications on the microcomputers they will use in their offices. Employees are required to pass competency tests on the use of the information technology used by Midwest as a condition of employment.

Midwest went through a change three years ago that let the sales reps working in Iowa have offices in their homes. There were 39 sales reps in Iowa and each had a home office furnished with phone lines, microcomputers, laser printers, fax capabilities, voice mail, and other features that you would normally find in the office space Midwest generally rented in a town. The cost of the equipment was approximately $6,500 per sales rep and the equipment was scheduled to be replaced every three years. The yearly cost for maintenance and repair of equipment, as well as other costs associated with the home office, was about $625 per year per salesman. This figure ($108,875 in total) was significantly less than the expense of having traditional offices in towns spread across Iowa.

All sales reps are required to complete a one week technology class every two years. A wide variety of topics are covered in the class. New fertilizers, genetically engineered crops, waste water recovery from livestock operations, and computer assisted farm management techniques are a few of the topics. The classes are not designed to make the sales reps experts in the topics covered, but rather to make them competent to discuss the topics with their customers.

Akron also provides one week classes in each of the topic areas that are designed to give sales reps in-depth knowledge of the subject. Bob had sent two of his sales reps to the waste water recovery class when a large hog slaughtering operation moved into the area serviced by his distribution center. That led directly to $24 million of sales to the firm since his sales reps were better trained to meet the slaughtering operation's needs.

Bob generally took one week classes in subjects he believed would yield high dollar sales. Waste water management, irrigation, and alternative fertilizers were the topics he focused on. Lucy had taken several classes on computerized farm management applications. Will concentrated on insect resistant seeds and genetically engineered crops. Midwest had a strong commitment to keeping its employees current with the technological changes in farming.

This year, for the first time, a one week class was offered on the use of information technology. The topics were of interest to Bob since he was the state director of the only state where Midwest Farm Supplies had an electronic office for every sales rep. The other states still had traditional "store front" offices in towns across the state. Those offices are well equipped with computer technology but the individual sales reps were merely computer literate, not proficient in the use of information technology.

Bob, Lucy, and Will are meeting in Akron this week to attend the class on information technology. The class is being taught by John Kubanna. John was promoted to the position of database administrator this year. He had been the distribution center liaison assigned to the two centers in Iowa and was responsible for purchasing and installing all of the computer equipment and peripheral devices in Iowa distribution centers. John's new duties include finding new ways to make better use of computing resources to support data access.

Bob Deer: It's good to see you again, John. We've been very pleased with the systems you set up for us last year. There have been improvements each year since we started in Iowa and so far we haven't had a serious problem.

John Kubanna: Some of that has been luck. There was the ice storm south of Indianapolis last year that took communications down for several days. Then the quality of the phone lines was poor and that caused problems with orders and other services. If that storm had been in Iowa instead of Indiana, then there could have been problems with your communications.

Bob Deer: What's the agenda for the information technology class this week?

John Kubanna: We'll be presenting some options for distribution centers to access our database. Used to be that everyone just dialed in as if their PC was a computer terminal and accessed the Akron database to process orders, look up prices, and so forth. Then we started using password protected web pages for these functions. Some of the changes this year are beginning to put a heavy load on our resources. When you take into account the added communications needed to support the changes, you end up with added expenses that grew a little too fast.

Lucy Rollins: This is a change in policy. How did these new policies increase the workload on the computer resources?

John Kubanna: Well, the first policy change was to use a "smart" program for capturing customer orders. That was a good position for Midwest to take. Every time a customer order is being placed, the order processing application checks the materials ordered the usual way to make sure they are in stock and other details. But it also checks to see if there are any items related to the ordered products that should be considered.

A customer orders PVC pipe and so the application prompts to see if the customer needs PVC cement or joints or a crimping tool. We've found that a lot of the larger orders are cleaner because everything gets ordered at once. Not PVC pipe on one order, a crimping tool on the next, and a third order for something else that was forgotten when the first order was placed. Those extra orders with low dollar volumes hurt.

It may sound like a simple thing, but we've found that sales revenues are up 15% and the net sales margins are up over 20%. Since we tend to process a large order once, instead of a dribble of three or four small orders, we have far lower ordering and shipping expenses to cover.

Will Kirk: I know what you mean. As I watch orders processed at Cedar Rapids I can see the effect it has on our customers. Besides just the dollars and cents figures here in Akron, the benefit in good customer relations is important. Probably more important than anything else.

This is a good way to impress our customers, we're seen as people who *really* know what we sell. And it's *true*. It was the knowledge of our sales reps that came up with the list of related items for an order. It's the good will generated and the demonstration of our expertise that keeps our customer base happy.

Lucy Rollins: I agree.

John Kubanna: But the order entry application takes longer to run because it has to wait for the customer and sales rep to discuss what they want to add to the order. A lot of times the sales rep is at the customer's farm and using a laptop with a wireless phone connection. The actual computer time is virtually the same, but the application program has to wait for the sales rep to enter an item, discuss something with the customer, enter another item, and so on.

Bob Deer: So the added cost is for communications?

John Kubanna: And database costs. The database we use now is a central server. Everybody who wants data from the database accesses it, uses an application program written for it, and uses communications lines to get to it. Centralization is good for security and it is usually more efficient.

Now that there are good computer resources at the distribution centers and with the sales reps in Iowa we have opportunities to improve information services. For example, Cedar Rapids and Cherokee both replace PCs on a three year cycle so they have all the needed computing and telecommunications power. Your applications run under Windows and we train all of your people here so we know their capabilities. These people are trained and equipped and ready to take advantage of more information technology.

I'd like to find a way to make better use of the computer resources here in Akron by making fuller use of the resources you have in the field. There is plenty of power in the distribution centers and in your sales reps laptop computers, it's just a question of accessing it.

Bob Deer: I've read some articles in trade journals about client-server databases. From the way they talked, I thought everybody either already had a client-server database or was about to get one.

John Kubanna: We've been thinking about the client-server structure. But we are like most companies, we have a system that works well and we don't want to change just to be part of the latest fad.

Bob Deer: Tell us more about client-server databases. Are they relational database management systems? How much does the software cost for a microcomputer? Do we have to learn a new language to access them?

John Kubanna: Client-server databases are a method of storing data for the database management system in one place and serving the data to applications on a client's computer. The terms relational and hierarchical refer to how data items are combined into database records and how the records are accessed. A client-server database essentially has a single database of information and a server computer processes the transactions from clients against the data in that database. Then it 'serves' the processed output to the client application. It just happens that the database management system we are thinking about for our client-server database is a relational database management system.

Right now if Lucy and Will are accessing the order processing application, then the microcomputers in their offices, at Cherokee and Cedar Rapids, don't process the data. The database is here in Akron, the database application (maybe a report or a database query) is here, and all of the computer processing for the transaction is here in Akron. Only the answer is sent back to their respective offices.

With a client-server structure there is only one database and that will be in Akron. But Lucy will have a copy of the order processing application on her computer in Cherokee. Will will have a copy of the same application on his computer in Cedar Rapids. Lucy needs some database information like the price and availability of a product. Along with that is a list of related items or products. That information is sent back to Cherokee for the application on her computer to assemble the order.

The good thing is that data is still stored once and only once. That way, it is secure and not likely to be corrupted. Only one computer, the Akron computer, actually changes the database values. You also make better use of your microcomputer. There's no sense making a powerful PC act like a dumb terminal. Might as well use its full capabilities.

Lucy Rollins: What about a distributed database structure? I remember reading that you can actually move parts of the database out to the areas where it is used. We use inventory and price items a lot, can't they be moved out to the field?

If Midwest used a distributed database architecture, wouldn't it be able to make even better use of the computer resources in the field? I mean, isn't it better to use several computers to be database servers than a single computer in Akron?

John Kubanna: It depends. I know that sounds like an evasive answer but you have to ask yourself if the pieces of the database are fairly separate.

The price list and inventory levels that are checked when an order is placed are the same ones whether you ask the question from Cedar Rapids or from Cherokee. Now some things are kept in stock at both locations and it seems reasonable to say that those things at your location should be on your own piece of the distributed database. But then it's company policy to check your own inventory first, but then to check the inventory of other sites. That process is simpler if all of the databases are kept in Akron.

Lucy Rollins: But we do a lot of applications other than order processing. We process payroll every month, pay our bills, send out mail for promotions, track individual customer purchase habits, and many other things.

John Kubanna: You are right. Since a customer is in one and only one service area, it doesn't require a centralized database to track purchase habits.

Bob Deer: And that is important. It doesn't make sense to simply have our sales reps waiting by the phone and hoping that someone will call. The sales reps have an application that sorts through key purchases and then makes estimates if the customer should be ready to reorder. If they don't call us, we call them!

When we find that a customer has ordered an insecticide with a four week potency and hasn't ordered another purchase of insecticide within a month, then we know we should make a call on that customer. Or a customer might have bought fence wire for a new section, that wire has a three year life and the customer can be contacted to seek a repeat sale.

John Kubanna: Those are good examples where the database is unique at each distribution center because a customer is a customer at only one center. It is the same application program, only the data processed by the application is different.

Will Kirk: What about our sales reps? Each of them has a microcomputer at his or her house. Could they run their application against their own set of customers? Their PCs should be powerful enough to handle the application.

Lucy Rollins: But a lot of customers might call into the distribution center as easily as the sales rep. Remember that the customer simply calls a 1-800 number. It's the phone system in Akron that determines where to route the call to reach the sales rep. And if the sales rep is not home to answer, the call the phone "bounces" to the distribution center.

No calls are lost. If they don't get a sales rep or a staff member at the distribution center, then a voice mail system kicks in to take a phone message. We're 99% sure of making a connection with the customer.

John Kubanna: But there is no need for a sales rep to keep a private list of customers. I mean, what if the sales rep was injured or took a vacation? How would Midwest service the customer if the database entries for that customer were on the sales rep's private computer? Since those are company records they should be somewhere that the company can easily access.

Bob Deer: Okay, let me see if I understand this. The costs for accessing company-wide applications, like order processing, are higher than they need to be. It's a lot more profitable to access a common "smart" order entry application than the way we used to do it. We made a good profit by strategically positioning Midwest with an order entry application that looks for products related to the ones the customer is ordering.

First, increase profits by knowing the profit potential of an information system. Then, go back and make the application more efficient so you can make even more profits. I like the way that works out.

Making the order entry and similar applications more efficient relies on making better use of computer resources in the field. There is a lot of unused computer power in the microcomputers we have on our desks. Besides that, it'll cut down on delays that occurred when we had to access data from Akron.

The trick seems to be to decide how to make the connection. Distributed database architectures keep multiple copies of the database at several sites. That data may not be consistent when several centers are processing stuff. I mean, Cherokee may sell most of Akron's inventory of fence wire and if Cedar Rapids has its own separate copy of the database then the Cherokee transaction may not get immediately reflected on the Cedar Rapids database.

A client-server architecture keeps copies of the application program, like the order processing application, at several sites, but only one database file exists. The application sites are the clients and the one database site is the server. The data is always correct.

John Kubanna: That's the general idea. Over the next few days I hope we can work on some possible answers. Choosing client-server or distributed database or something else requires some careful thought. Who knows, maybe we should just keep going the way we are. Some people say, "If it isn't broken, don't fix it." But I just don't think that's a good idea when it comes to computer applications.

Information systems technology is changing fast and everybody is getting more computer literate. It seems that if you aren't running forward then your competition is running past you.

QUESTIONS:

1. Describe computer literacy. Explain why Midwest Farm Supplies needs staff that are proficient in the use of information technology, not merely literate, in order to be more efficient and effective.

2. Client-server databases rely on data that is centralized and applications that use that data can be dispersed in many locations in the organization. How has the availability of powerful, inexpensive microcomputers helped make client-server databases possible?

3. The "smart" computer programs in the case are actually expert systems. Explain how the knowledge of tasks performed by sales reps is important to the development of an expert system for sales orders. Use examples from the case.

4. A key consideration in the distributed database versus client-server database question is whether or not the information on the database is needed by a single site or multiple sites. Use the sales ordering system to justify either a distributed database or client-server database for Midwest Farm Supplies.

McLeod / Schell Case Solution Form 1
The Problem Setting

Case: <u>Midwest Farm Supplies</u>   **Name:** _____

Environmental Elements:

Important Facts:

McLeod / Schell Case Solution Form 2
Elements of the Firm as a System

Case: <u>Midwest Farm Supplies</u>   **Name:** _____

Objectives and/or Standards:

Output:

Management and Organization:

Information Processor:

Inputs and Input Resources:

Transformation Process:

Output Resources:

McLeod / Schell Case Solution Form 3
Subsystems of the Firm

Case: **Midwest Farm Supplies**   **Name:** _____

Subsystem:

Subsystem:

Subsystem:

Subsystem:

McLeod / Schell Case Solution Form 4
Problems and Symptoms

Case: <u>Midwest Farm Supplies</u>   **Name:** _____

Environment:
Objectives and/or Standards:
Output:
Management and Organization:
Information Processor:
Inputs and Physical System:

Main Problem(s):

1.

2.

3.

McLeod / Schell Case Solution Form 5
Alternatives

Case: <u>Midwest Farm Supplies</u>　　　　　**Name:** _____

Alternative:

  Advantages:

  Disadvantages:

Alternative:

  Advantages:

  Disadvantages:

McLeod / Schell Case Solution Form 5
Alternatives

Case: <u>Midwest Farm Supplies</u>   **Name:** _____

Alternative:

  Advantages:

  Disadvantages:

Alternative:

  Advantages:

  Disadvantages:

McLeod / Schell Case Solution Form 6
Decision and Implementation

Case: Midwest Farm Supplies　　　　　Name: _____

Decision:

Implementation Resources Needed:

Implementation Steps to be Followed:

CAMPUS BOOKSTORE

Leslie University (LU) is a private, four-year university with over 12,000 students. The university was founded in Huron, South Dakota by a grant from Leslie Schumacher in 1961. The university offers degrees in history, political science, nursing, business, biology, and other areas. Virtually all of the texts used at LU are sold through the campus bookstore.

Campus bookstores are frequently the focus of criticism from students and faculty. The common complaints are that the prices are too high, that texts needed for classes are not in stock on time or that the supply runs out, and that the prices paid to students selling their texts back to the bookstore are not fair. Some of the criticism is justified, but some is not.

The bookstore at LU was founded when the university was established. Its original mission was to identify sources of texts and secure enough of them to meet the demands of the faculty and students. Over the years the mission changed. The campus grew from several hundred students to thousands. The needs of the students and faculty changed and the bookstore changed with them.

The bookstore offers a number of services. Its primary purpose is to sell and repurchase texts. It also sells pencils, pens, souvenirs, clothing, computers, and many other items. It serves as a check cashing facility for students and an automated teller machine is located by its front door. The bookstore has acquired responsibilities in many areas of student life that are far removed from its original mission.

The bookstore is managed by Rick Holly. Joe Crowne is the assistant manager for texts and Peggy Jones is the assistant manager for student services. Joe is responsible for all functions relating to texts and for course related materials such as laboratory supplies, art supplies, and other materials. Peggy is responsible for all other areas, but most of her time is used to manage sales of clothing and general school supplies. Rick has the overall responsibility for the bookstore's operations. He supervises Joe and Peggy and directly administers all personnel functions of bookstore employees such as hiring and raises.

The bookstore must order texts for each course offered. Courses are offered on a semester basis (Fall and Spring and two compressed semesters are offered each summer). Over 600 courses are offered in each of the Spring and Fall semesters and approximately 100 courses are offered in each of the summer semesters. Almost 400 publishers supplied the texts for the 1,400 courses last year, although almost 90% of texts come from less than 25 publishers.

Text order forms are sent to faculty members ten weeks before the course begins. Faculty are supposed to complete the form showing the text title, author, edition, publisher, and the number of texts needed. There is additional space for written comments such as "this text is suggested but not required." Text orders are required to be returned to the bookstore eight weeks before classes begin.

Most students at LU preregister for their courses, e.g. they register for Spring courses while they are still taking Fall courses. About 20 percent of registrations occur the week before classes begin. These are usually transfer students, but some students miss their preregistration appointments. It is difficult to predict the courses in which transfer students will register.

The orders for texts are due in the bookstore the week before preregistration occurs. This means faculty are forced to guess the student enrollment in their classes. The preregistration enrollments are not considered when the faculty member estimates enrollment because those figures are not available until after the text order form has been sent to the bookstore.

The campus has a "suggestion box" that solicits ideas from faculty, students, and staff on ways to improve LU. Each month, one suggestion is selected as the most important and the winner is given a prize. The prizes awarded vary according to the recipient. Students generally receive a semester's worth of texts at no charge. Staff can win gift certificates up to $300 for clothing and other bookstore items. Faculty receive a $10 gift certificate.

Helen Ibarra is a professor in the business school who teaches information systems courses. She could not understand the reason for ordering texts so early. If the forms could be sent a week later, then her enrollment estimate would be much more accurate. Only the number of transfer students would change enrollment estimates. That was a much smaller problem than estimating the entire number of students in a course. And determining the number of texts to order was very important to the bookstore since many complaints were about too few texts and too many students.

The university has a computerized enrollment procedure. It is part of a complete student information system that encompasses course schedules, transcripts, enforcement of course prerequisites, and many other features. Helen realized that enrollment figures could be retrieved from the student information system instead of requiring faculty to guess the numbers and place them on the form. In Helen's opinion, the form should have title, author, edition, and other text information. The number of texts to be ordered could be generated from the preregistration enrollment figures.

Helen made this suggestion through the suggestion program. She cited the benefits: better service to students, dollar savings for the bookstore, and more convenience for the faculty. The suggestion won that month's prize and Helen won a $10 gift certificate. The chancellor of the university wrote Helen a letter praising her suggestion because of its savings for the university and service to the students. There was a strong suggestion in the letter that Helen should work with the bookstore to devise a plan to implement the suggestion.

Helen arranged a meeting with Joe to discuss her suggestion and learn more about the system the bookstore was currently using. There was a certain amount of tension before the meeting took place. The bookstore had been harassed and ridiculed by faculty for some time. Faculty complained that the bookstore was poorly managed each time it would run out of a text. There was a feeling that the prices charged were too high considering that the bookstore was supposed to service the students.

The bookstore was no fan of the faculty. The faculty complained bitterly when too few books arrived to meet student needs. But the faculty seldom estimated the number of students correctly. To make matters worse, they frequently changed the text they wanted for a course and often didn't give the bookstore all the information necessary to place the order. Helen felt the meeting would be civil, but there was a history of bad feelings between the bookstore and the faculty concerning text orders.

Helen Ibarra: Thanks for coming. I didn't realize that Rick would be here also.

Joe Crowne: Well, I'm responsible for the text ordering systems, but he has responsibility for the operations of the bookstore. If we decide to make any significant changes from the current system, Rick will have to approve them.

Helen Ibarra: The system we have just doesn't work.

Joe Crowne: We ordered almost 150,000 texts last year. That's a pretty big job. You only have to worry about the classes you teach.

Helen Ibarra: Ordering the texts would be simpler if you just let the information systems that are already in place do some of the work. The student information system keeps track of enrollments. You don't need for faculty to make estimates of enrollments before registration takes place, just take the enrollments from the student information system.

Rick Holly: We can't do that.

Helen Ibarra: Why not?

Rick Holly: The student information system is under the control of the registrar's office. They use it for a variety of applications from considering financial aid to accepting or rejecting enrollment applications to recording transcripts. They feel that giving us access to the system would risk the confidentiality of the student records.

Helen Ibarra: Only if they allow access to sensitive information. The student information system is designed as a series of screens. One screen shows enrollments in courses. It is the only screen you need and does not contain confidential material.
Every user is assigned a list of one or more screens that they are allowed to access. You could be limited to the one screen displaying class enrollment sizes.

Rick Holly: I know.

Helen Ibarra: So why don't you have the registrar's office give you an account on the student information system that provides access to course enrollments.

Rick Holly: We've asked several times but we've never been approved. They always justify their decision on the privacy issue.

Helen Ibarra: That just doesn't make sense. There is no privacy that could be violated by telling you how many students are in a course. The system has a screen display that gives only enrollment totals, no names are provided. Any taxpayer in the state can walk into the registrar's office and demand that information. The registrar is required by law to give the information to the taxpayer. How can they refuse to give the information to you?

Rick Holly: Good question.

Helen Ibarra: Okay, let's assume that the registrar's office will be persuaded to provide access to the computerized enrollment totals. Can you explain the process you use now to order texts?

Joe Crowne: The process requires a lot of lead time for several reasons. First, we need the time to canvass text wholesalers about our purchases. The wholesalers sell used texts and their costs are greatly reduced from new text prices. But we have to order early because we compete against other schools. The schools that begin their semester the earliest are the ones with the advantage.
    The wholesalers do not take returns, we can only resell the books back to them. That's at a much reduced price, about 60 cents on the dollar. The publisher has a "free return" policy that isn't really free, but it is much more forgiving than the wholesalers' policies. Publishers charge a restocking fee of 5 to 15 percent of the text price.
    Another reason for the long lead time is manpower. The university doesn't provide full time employee status to the work of book order entry. That means we have to use students and other part-time help to enter book order data. Sometimes we have a full-time staff member enter the data, because they can do it much faster, and the part-time employee takes over the full-time employee's tasks in the mean time. Our budget allocation is low and the university constrains us to use part-time employees approximately the same number of hours each week. So we have too little work for them almost the whole semester, then too much work when we need to process textbook orders.

Helen Ibarra: Let me interrupt a second. The texts that are going to be used the next semester are known soon after the current semester begins. The course schedule is made well in advance. The course schedule for the Spring semester, which starts in January, is made in September. The Summer and Fall schedules are made in early March.
    There are some course changes and you don't know every text needed, but almost all text decisions are made when the schedule is made. If we (faculty) sent the text decisions to the bookstore when the course schedules were made, you would have plenty of time to get the data entered long before registration starts.
    You could use enrollment figures from the computerized registration process to fill in the information about how many texts to order. That could be done at a later time. That would spread your manpower requirements over a much longer period. You wouldn't be in a crunch to get text information entered into the computer. You'd probably be able to make arrangements with the text wholesalers sooner.

Rick Holly: You are assuming that the registrar's office will allow the bookstore to access the registration figures generated by the student information system.

Helen Ibarra: Yes, I think we can make a compelling case. There seems to be a terrible communications breakdown about how texts are ordered.

Joe Crowne: The only communication we ever receive is a complaint. No faculty member has ever asked how the texts are ordered. They say, "That's not my problem" and demand that their text orders are always available, no matter how late they request it or how inaccurate their estimated enrollment might be.
    Continuing on my reasons for the long lead time, once we know which texts are going to be used again, the books from wholesalers are ordered. Then we subtract the number of used texts that we can get from the wholesaler and from students from the total number of texts reported on the text order from. We only order texts from the publisher if we cannot get them from the wholesaler. The wholesaler is cheaper.
    The publishers have a professional association that gives us free software and a database so that we can identify every text quickly. All of it runs on a personal computer. Part of the application package is an

electronic data interchange (EDI) system that connects our personal computer to the order system of the publisher of the text. No written forms are required. Well, it's not really an EDI system, we use a special phone number from our modem to make a connection to the EDI system so I guess the communication between us and the first link isn't on the EDI system.

Helen Ibarra: So everything from the publishers' view is completely computerized?

Rick Holly: We probably deal with 15 publishers in a year that are not members of the association. Those are typically authors who decide to publish their own text instead of using an established publisher. We can easily deal with those few publishers manually.

Joe Crowne: We keep track of enrollment figures from past semesters and we make estimates about the enrollments for the upcoming semester.

Helen Ibarra: Which underscores the absurdity that the registrar will not give you access to those figures as enrollment progresses.
    It seems that the only data you really need to gather close to the end of the semester is the enrollment figures. All of the other text information can be made available long before texts would have to be ordered, while you have enough staff to enter the data into your computers. What are your real time constraints?

Joe Crowne: The orders have to go through the system 11 days before they are to arrive on campus. We need to have repurchased all the books that the bookstore is going to buy back from students 16 days before the semester begins.

Helen Ibarra: Right now you are basing decisions about ordering texts from wholesalers and publishers from information that is just a faculty member's guess that occurs before registration starts. Your orders would be far more accurate if you used the enrollment figures from the registration files.

Rick Holly: But we need to finalize our orders from the wholesalers three weeks before the semester starts.

Helen Ibarra: Three weeks is much better than the current eight to twelve weeks. Faculty are now required to guess at enrollments eight weeks before the semester starts. We have a much more accurate picture after the preregistration process is over.
    We still won't know the exact enrollments because late registration takes place the week before the semester begins and students can drop and add classes during the first week of class. But I think we would do a much better job.

Rick Holly: What is "better?"

Helen Ibarra: What do you mean?

Rick Holly: Who gets to define "better?"

Helen Ibarra: "Better" is more accurate estimates of how many texts to order.

Rick Holly: What about price? What about decisions concerning how many texts to buy back from students?

Helen Ibarra: Those are good questions, but I have a class in ten minutes. I think we've made some real progress today, but I think we've gone as far as we can until the registrar's office gives permission to let you access the class enrollment figures.

Joe Crowne: I think you're right.

Rick Holly: It's been unusual talking with a faculty member that is rational. I think if we had received some cooperation before we could have saved a lot of headaches.

Helen agreed to meet with Joe and Rick at the bookstore in two weeks. She would be given a demonstration of text ordering. The introductory management information systems class she taught would cover electronic data interchange in three weeks and she would have Joe Crowne provide a demonstration of the publisher association's system.

The registrar's office provided Rick with an account on the student information system. It seems that the request had always been turned down by the clerk in charge of establishing the account because the request was not approved by a senior administration official. Several years earlier, in an attempt to insure student privacy, the administration had established a policy that only faculty could have accounts on the student information system since the faculty were responsible for grading, advising, and similar functions. A staff request required permission from a senior administrator.

The administration discovered later that the student information system could provide separate access to appropriate staff that would not compromise student privacy. The policy was changed so that appropriate staff could gain access to the student information system. Unfortunately, the paperwork never found its way to the clerk who established the accounts. The staff at the bookstore had never formally challenged the rejection of establishing the account. If they had, the clerk's error would have been discovered much sooner.

Rick demonstrated his skills on the student information system for Helen. Rick also accessed the student information system and could navigate to check the enrollments for specific sections. Both Rick and Joe could use the publisher association's software like experts. The software had a feature that would estimate the next semester's enrollment in a course based upon enrollment in previous semesters.

The enrollment projection in the publishers' software was quite sophisticated. It considered population trends, growth factors in different regions of the country, high course enrollments that could be expected if the course had not been offered recently, and many other features. The enrollment projections were accurate within 10 percent for most of the classes, but the program could make large errors for some courses.

During the last Fall semester the program made poor projections for 73 of the 600 classes. Joe and Rick could identify most of the courses where enrollments would not be accurately projected. They represented courses where the curriculum had changed or where few previous enrollments were available. Joe and Rick reviewed the requests for changes in curriculum each semester and made their best estimates concerning how the changed curriculum would affect enrollments.

Helen was surprised at the computer capabilities of Joe and Rick. She was also impressed with their understanding of the models used to predict enrollment figures. They generally predicted the order amounts within 10 books and seldom made a mistake greater than 25 books. She noticed that almost all of the errors were overestimates, few were low.

Helen Ibarra: Why are so few of your estimates low?

Rick Holly: Because the only times we get complaints are when we run out of a text. We look at the estimates from the model and then use our judgment to add texts to an order if we think the model might not provide a sufficient number of texts. Nobody complains when we have too many texts.

I see what you are getting at. But don't worry much about the wholesalers' texts or books we get from students. They sell us used texts and those are almost always sold. New texts are the ones that might be left over.

An example could be the statistics text that was used last semester. We bought 115 used texts from wholesalers, 248 from students, and 185 new texts from the publisher. All of the used texts sold but we had 27 new texts that weren't sold. Students almost always buy the cheaper, used texts first.

Helen Ibarra: Would the bookstore care if students exchanged used books among themselves? The prices you charge for used books are still pretty high and students get very little for their used texts.

Joe Crowne: That's right. But most people don't realize our charter actually prohibits us from making profits on texts. Each year we estimate our mark-up in order to cover expenses. And our estimates are a little high since we have no source of funds to run the text side of the operations if we cannot cover expenses. So the excess money at the end of the year goes to Bookstore Scholarships. It's a program we have that distributes any excess revenue back to students in the form of scholarship money to be used to purchase texts.

As far as used books, we just operate to cover our marginal costs. Since we don't have the manpower needed to physically move the books around the bookstore, we use workers from a temp agency. That costs us about $11 per hour for each person. They receive the books from students, check the books to make sure all pages are in the text, see if software sold with the text is still there, verify the text is in good condition, and a host of other things.

Then the used books have to be sorted, taken to the shelves where they are matched to courses, stocked, and so forth. Combined with that are all the normal expenses of entering a book into the inventory accounts, selling the books, and other general accounting tasks. It costs from $12 to $15 per used text just to process it into the bookstore and out again.

Helen Ibarra: So you wouldn't care if students worked out a system for exchanging texts among themselves?

Rick Holly: I wish they would. It would get rid of a lot of hassles and angry students who don't understand how much it costs to get the used books into stock and then out to be bought.

Helen Ibarra: I think students could run a system easily as long as the system just matched buyers to sellers and didn't have to handle payments or hold inventories of texts.

Rick Holly: We could too, but the bookstore doesn't have that luxury.

Joe Crowne: I could work with some of your information systems majors in the business school if you like. Their club could make the text exchange a service project or a fund raiser. Maybe charge 50 cents for each book a student wants to list on the exchange. The business school could start the ball rolling to see if a student exchange for used textbooks would really work. Then maybe expand to the other schools in the university. Who knows, maybe I'll be working for one of the students in five years.

Helen Ibarra: I like the idea. I think this would be a good project for my class this semester. We could have a trial implementation with the class to work out any bugs.

Rick Holly: With the majority of used texts swapped among the students themselves you'll find we need information about texts only about three weeks before the end of the semester. And with the return policies for new texts being so much more liberal than for used texts, we don't even need to be as accurate with our estimates. Students get cheaper texts, faculty don't have to give us enrollment estimates, and we don't have to hassle with so many used texts. This seems like a dream.

QUESTIONS:

1. Access to information can be hindered by the organization's procedures or by staff that misinterpret the procedures. What would you do to correct the situation in this case where a clerk denied the bookstore's request for an account?

2. Many areas of an organization may rely upon a single information system. How would you insure that all areas affected by an information system are fairly represented in its design and use?

3. Rick Holly seems very optimistic at the end of the case. What problems could still make the ordering of textbooks a difficult task?

4. Helen Ibarra and Rick Holly seem to feel that students could design and implement a system to broker the exchange of used textbooks. Explain how you would make such a system work. Would students enter their own information or would it be entered by information systems majors? Could forms be added to a web page for wide access? How would monies be collected and texts exchanged?

5. If the bookstore could use the publisher association's software to estimate enrollments, why did the bookstore ask faculty to provide enrollment estimates?

McLeod / Schell Case Solution Form 1
The Problem Setting

Case: <u>Campus Bookstore</u>　　　　　**Name:** _____

Environmental Elements:

Important Facts:

McLeod / Schell Case Solution Form 2
Elements of the Firm as a System

Case: Campus Bookstore   **Name:** _____

Objectives and/or Standards:

Output:

Management and Organization:

Information Processor:

Inputs and Input Resources:

Transformation Process:

Output Resources:

McLeod / Schell Case Solution Form 3
Subsystems of the Firm

Case: Campus Bookstore   **Name:** _____

Subsystem:

Subsystem:

Subsystem:

Subsystem:

McLeod / Schell Case Solution Form 4
Problems and Symptoms

Case: **Campus Bookstore**   Name: _____

Environment:
Objectives and/or Standards:
Output:
Management and Organization:
Information Processor:
Inputs and Physical System:

Main Problem(s):

1.

2.

3.

McLeod / Schell Case Solution Form 5
Alternatives

Case: Campus Bookstore   Name: _____

Alternative:

  Advantages:

  Disadvantages:

Alternative:

  Advantages:

  Disadvantages:

McLeod / Schell Case Solution Form 5
Alternatives

Case: <u>Campus Bookstore</u>　　　　　　　**Name:** _____

Alternative:

　Advantages:

　Disadvantages:

Alternative:

　Advantages:

　Disadvantages:

McLeod / Schell Case Solution Form 6
Decision and Implementation

Case: <u>Campus Bookstore</u>   **Name:** _____

Decision:

Implementation Resources Needed:

Implementation Steps to be Followed:

CANADIAN DATA SYSTEMS, Ltd.

Canadian Data Systems (CDS) is one of Canada's largest manufacturers of electronic office equipment. Headquartered in Quebec, CDS has plants in Quebec, Vancouver, Calgary, Regina, Winnipeg, and Toronto, and sales offices around the world. The company was founded in the early 1950s to supply key-driven bookkeeping machines to the Canadian banking industry. As the computer boom gained momentum in the 1960s, the electromechanical bookkeeping machines lost their sales appeal--first to electronic office machines and then to computers.

Organizational Structure

The bookkeeping machines have long since been withdrawn from the product line, but the office products are still being manufactured at the Calgary and Winnipeg plants, and marketed by all of the CDS sales offices. Included in the office products are copying machines, postage machines, mailing machines, desktop calculators, electronic typewriters, and facsimile transmission (FAX) machines. The computer line has grown to a family of systems that includes laptops, microcomputers, and minicomputers. All of the computer products are manufactured at the Quebec, Vancouver, Regina, and Toronto plants, and are marketed worldwide.

The two main product categories, office products and computers, form the basis for the CDS organizational structure as shown in Figure 1. Reporting to Roger Edens, the president, are two senior vice presidents. Jack Scott has responsibility for the office products division and Anne Marlowe plays the same role for the computer products division. For all practical purposes, the two divisions operate as separate companies, with each having its own objectives, strategic plan, fiscal budget, and functional areas of manufacturing, marketing, and finance. Each functional area is headed up by a vice president. For example, in the computer products division, Wiley Mangrum is vice president of manufacturing, Gene Washington is vice president of marketing, and Darla Brand is vice president of finance.

Also reporting to Edens is another senior vice president, the controller Sally Shepherd. Sally is responsible for three organizational units that provide services to the two divisions and stockholders. The accounting and information systems (IS) divisions support both the office products and computer products divisions, and the corporate relations office provides an interface with the firm's stockholders.

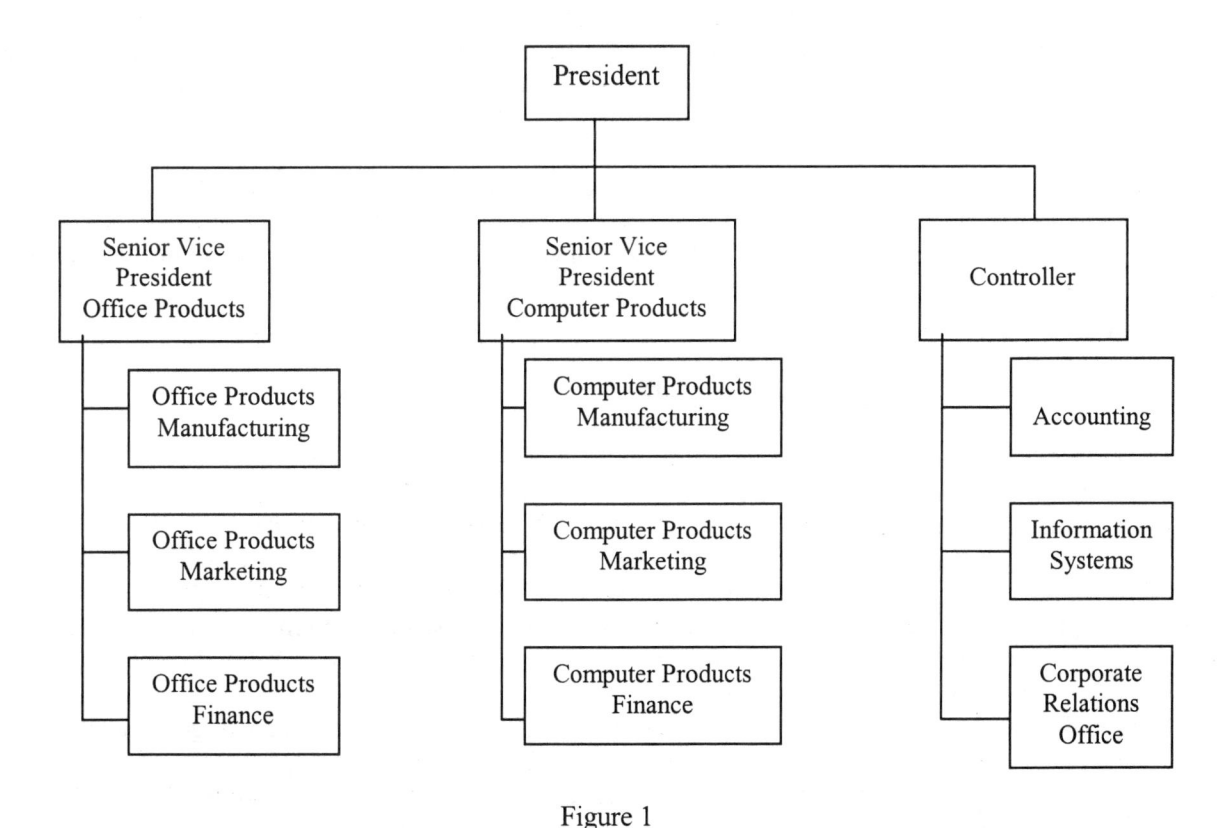

Figure 1

The CDS Organizational Structure

Strategic Planning

Edens and the three senior vice presidents compose the CDS executive committee, which establishes company policy, performs strategic planning, and makes key decisions. The CDS strategic business plan, which is updated each year, provides direction for the entire organization for the coming eight years. During the process of preparing the strategic business plan, the executive committee calls on the help of top-level managers from the subsidiary units. For example, Alton Fox, the vice president of information systems, provides input concerning the level of support that can be expected from his area.

In addition to the strategic business plan, the executive committee also assembles strategic plans for the major organizational units--the two product divisions, accounting, and IS. There is a strategic office products plan, a strategic computer products plan, a strategic plan for accounting resources, and a strategic plan for information resources. Most of the executive attention is directed at the two product plans, with the accounting and information resources plans taking the form of lists of future systems projects with general descriptions of the levels of resources required for each. Although each vice president is primarily responsible for the strategic plan for his or her area, all of the vice presidents work together to ensure that their plans are coordinated. As Alton Fox prepares the strategic plan for information resources, he works closely with Jack Scott, Anne Marlowe, and Sally Shepherd.

Information Systems

Although CDS was one of the early entrants in the computing industry, the development of information systems within the company did not take on much importance until approximately ten years ago. The reasons for the CDS lag in computer applications were:

1. The original product line, consisting of bookkeeping machines, was oriented toward data processing. As the company sought to establish itself as a role model for its customers, the emphasis was on the efficient processing of data rather than the preparation of management information.
2. Most of the early CDS executives rose through the ranks of the production side of the business where the emphasis was on the management of the physical, rather than informational, resources.
3. The information that was needed for the production of the electromechanical bookkeeping machines was well defined and easily obtainable since all of the assembly processes were performed at the single Quebec plant. Manufacturing managers typically managed by observation, rather than by using formal reporting systems.

The decision in the mid-1960s to enter the potentially lucrative computer market signaled the end of the simplified production processes that had characterized the bookkeeping machines, and, to a lesser extent, the office machines. When the computer line was added, the number of component parts in a finished product increased by a factor of a hundred, the component parts became much more complex, and the production process was no longer the relatively simple assembly of mechanical parts.

Computer Applications in the Computer Products Division

Because of the increased complexity of the computer production process, the manufacturing function of the computer products division became the first big computer user within CDS. A material requirements planning (MRP) system was implemented, followed by an upgrading to a manufacturing resource planning (MRP-II) system. More recently, the computer products manufacturing managers decided to use mathematical models to determine the optimum locations of manufacturing equipment at their plants and to arrange the layouts of the plant floors. The location of the Regina plant and its layout had been determined through mathematical modeling. The positive effect of the Regina layout on efficiency was so dramatic that the executive committee decided that modeling should be used to revise the layouts of the other plants as well.

The modeling success of the computer products manufacturing function did not go unnoticed by the marketing function. When computer products marketing asked IS to look into the use of modeling in the sales area, the development of the marketing budget was identified as an ideal application. Members of the marketing staff worked with IS in designing a mathematical model that uses the sales representatives' sales forecasts to project the numbers and types of computer products that CDS will sell during the coming year. This sales projection provides the basis for determining the resources that will be needed in both marketing and manufacturing. For example, the model identifies the number of salespersons and company cars, types of office equipment and supplies, and so on that will be needed to meet the forecast. Marketing makes its resource projections available to the computer products finance function where they are used in computing the marketing operating budget. The computer products marketing function began using this model, called the marketing planning model, in June of 1993, and it has worked like a charm. It relieves marketing managers and staff of many laborious calculations.

The use of computers by the computer products division has made it the envy of the rest of the company. By taking advantage of the company's information resources, the computer products division has been able to continually increase its sales revenue and, at the same time, keep expenses in line. In 1994 almost two-thirds of the CDS profits came from computer products and the proportion has increased until almost 85% of profits come from computer products today.

Computer Products Marketing

The computer products marketing function is organized along the lines of the chart in Figure 2. Nine managers report to the functional vice president, Gene Washington. Five of the managers are regional sales managers, three are product managers, and there is a manager of marketing research.

The regional sales managers are responsible for sales in their particular areas. Ancel Cluff is located in Quebec, Carter Greer in Chicago, Charley Hinkle in Tokyo, Cecil Hewey in London, and Diana Stinson in Frankfurt. Each regional office includes the sales representatives for that area, and the representatives report directly to the regional manager.

The product managers are responsible for coordinating all of the activities that go into the production of their particular products. Gordon Luckey is responsible for laptops, Marsha Hill for microcomputers, and Penney Berry for minicomputers (CDS minicomputers are often used as web servers).

John Stearns is the most recent addition to the marketing management team. He was hired three years ago to head up the marketing research department after having built an impressive track record in a similar position with a Chicago newspaper.

The three product managers, along with Cluff and Stearns, have their offices in the Quebec corporate headquarters and they seldom travel. Washington and the regional sales managers, on the other hand, are constantly on the move. At one time the travel created havoc with communications and the managers spent a lot of time playing "telephone tag." That problem was solved with electronic mail and cellular phones. Each manager has a laptop equipped with a wireless modem via the cell phone. Regardless of where the regional managers are, they can always communicate by e-mail. The other members of the computer products marketing staff also use e-mail to communicate with their contacts in the plants, sales offices, and headquarters.

All of the marketing managers have networked micros in their offices and use them primarily for communications. The managers know the importance of good communications to sales. The quick, accurate exchange of the right information is often the difference between success and failure.

The Strategic Plan for Information Resources

Although CDS got a late start in establishing its information systems operation, the computer resources are impressive. An IBM mainframe computer performs most of the processing, and is supported by less powerful minicomputers produced by CDS and several other manufacturers. One computer, produced by Dell, is used primarily for communicating data between the headquarters and the plant and office sites. Each plant and regional sales office is included in the CDS data communications network.

In addition, there are a large number of the company's own minis and micros scattered throughout headquarters, plants, and regional offices. CDS uses computers manufactured by some of its competitors for two reasons. First, CDS wants to fully understand the products sold by competitors and there is no better way to understand a product than to use the product. Second, IBM and Dell both act as manufacturers for computer subcomponents used in CDS products.

The executive committee believes that since CDS is in the computer business it should set a good example for computer use. To achieve this objective, the committee has provided a guiding framework in the form of the strategic plan for information resources, supported by the necessary policies and procedures. The overriding policy is one of maintaining central control over computer use while at the same time encouraging end-user computing. The policy dictates that development of new applications for organizational information systems be approved and controlled by the MIS steering committee. Organizational information systems are those that support the entire CDS organization--the accounting information system (AIS), management information system (MIS), decision support systems, and certain office automation (OA) designs. Organizational OA systems are implemented company-wide and include electronic mail, voice mail, video conferencing, and multimedia projects.

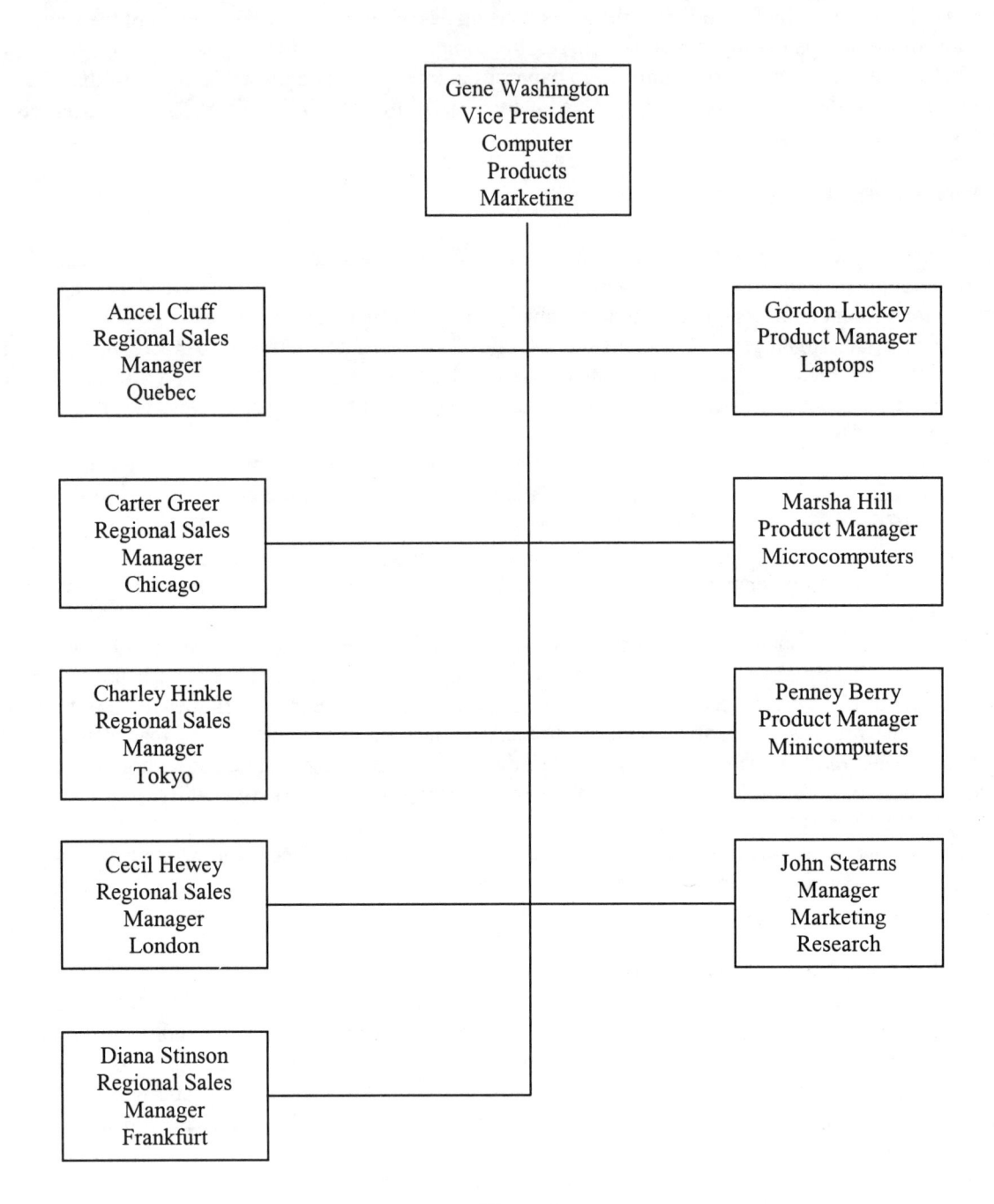

```
                        ┌──────────────────┐
                        │ Gene Washington  │
                        │ Vice President   │
                        │ Computer         │
                        │ Products         │
                        │ Marketing        │
                        └──────────────────┘
                                 │
    ┌──────────────────┐         │         ┌──────────────────┐
    │ Ancel Cluff      │         │         │ Gordon Luckey    │
    │ Regional Sales   │─────────┼─────────│ Product Manager  │
    │ Manager          │         │         │ Laptops          │
    │ Quebec           │         │         │                  │
    └──────────────────┘         │         └──────────────────┘
                                 │
    ┌──────────────────┐         │         ┌──────────────────┐
    │ Carter Greer     │         │         │ Marsha Hill      │
    │ Regional Sales   │─────────┼─────────│ Product Manager  │
    │ Manager          │         │         │ Microcomputers   │
    │ Chicago          │         │         │                  │
    └──────────────────┘         │         └──────────────────┘
                                 │
    ┌──────────────────┐         │         ┌──────────────────┐
    │ Charley Hinkle   │         │         │ Penney Berry     │
    │ Regional Sales   │─────────┼─────────│ Product Manager  │
    │ Manager          │         │         │ Minicomputers    │
    │ Tokyo            │         │         │                  │
    └──────────────────┘         │         └──────────────────┘
                                 │
    ┌──────────────────┐         │         ┌──────────────────┐
    │ Cecil Hewey      │         │         │ John Stearns     │
    │ Regional Sales   │─────────┼─────────│ Manager          │
    │ Manager          │         │         │ Marketing        │
    │ London           │         │         │ Research         │
    └──────────────────┘         │         └──────────────────┘
                                 │
    ┌──────────────────┐         │
    │ Diana Stinson    │         │
    │ Regional Sales   │─────────┘
    │ Manager          │
    │ Frankfurt        │
    └──────────────────┘
```

Figure 2

The Computer Products Division Marketing Management Staff

The MIS steering committee includes the members of the executive committee plus the vice president of information systems, Fox. To guide the MIS steering committee in managing the development process of organizational systems, the executive committee established the formal procedure described below.

1. Requests for development of a new, modified, or reengineered system will be described on the IS Project Request Form. The form will be supported by a network diagram documenting the planned development process, a preliminary cost analysis following the established guidelines, and a designation of the project leader. The project leader will be the manager who will have responsibility for the system. The team will include at least one member from the internal auditing department.
2. The MIS steering committee will review all project requests and determine whether they should be approved or rejected.
3. During the development process of approved projects, the project leader will submit weekly written reports to the MIS steering committee and meet with the committee when requested. The purpose of the reports is to compare actual progress to the plan, explain any variations, and describe the activity for the coming week.
4. At the end of the planning, analysis, design, and implementation phases, the project leader will submit the system documentation to the vice president of information systems for approval. The documentation is expected to meet the CDS standards for documentation, built-in systems controls, and security precautions. When the vice president of information systems is satisfied that the system is ready for implementation, he or she will advise the MIS steering committee in writing.
5. No later than 90 days after implementation of the system, the project leader will have all system users complete the CDS Postimplementation Review Form as a way of measuring the degree of user satisfaction. The manager of internal auditing will also conduct a postimplementation review. The project leader and manager of internal auditing will summarize their findings in a written report that will be provided to the MIS steering committee. The committee will determine the need for follow-up action.
6. The postimplementation review process will be repeated on an annual basis for the life of the system, with the vice president of information systems summarizing the content of the postimplementation review forms.

Systems that are not meant to support the entire organization are another matter. These systems support individual users or small work groups, and good examples include decision support systems (DSSs) that do not have an organizational focus. In permitting a less strict development process for these systems, the executive committee not only encourages end-user computing, but also the use of CDS products.

The development of applications to support individuals or work groups can be approved and managed at the functional level. This means, for example, that if someone in computer products marketing wants to implement a DSS or an individual OA application, he or she must only obtain approval from Gene Washington, the vice president of marketing in the computer products division. Washington would then have the responsibility to monitor the development to ensure that it goes properly in terms of documentation, security, and system controls. In managing and controlling its information resources, CDS, therefore, follows a top-down policy for organizational systems, and a bottom-up policy for individual and work group systems.

Computer Use by Computer Products Managers

Although the managers of the computer products division are the biggest users of computer information, much of the use has been restricted to mathematical models that make programmed decisions. The MRP-II application, for example, simulates material consumption by the production system during the period covered by the production schedule, and the plant location and layout models determine the optimum arrangements of the physical resources at the plant sites. All of these models operate within well-defined parameters. The marketing planning model fits into this category as well, consisting of relatively simple calculations.

These mathematical models draw heavily on the database maintained by the accounting information system. The mainframe manages the database and performs all of the data processing applications of the accounting information system such as inventory, billing, and payroll. The mainframe also serves as the computer platform for the management information system, which produces hundreds of periodic reports that reflect various aspects of the firm's operations.

A proposed executive information system will be a subset of the MIS and will enable top-level managers to retrieve reports from networked micros located in their offices. Preformatted information that is tailored to the executive's information profile is downloaded from the database each day. In addition, each display will identify one or more persons in the organization who are expert on the particular information, in the event that the executive wishes a clarification or amplification of the report content.

The corporate database management system used on the mainframe includes query and report writer options that make it possible for managers throughout the company to obtain information on demand. The database management system purchased also allows these same query and report options to be performed on the executive's microcomputer. However, the managers have not seen fit to take advantage of this capability for producing special reports. Fox has recognized this void in the decision support provided by IS and plans to offer classes to CDS managers on the special reporting capabilities of the CDS hardware and software. Fox hopes that these classes will provide the stimulus necessary for managers to add special reports to their established use of periodic reports, simulation outputs, and electronic communications.

The Marketing Information System

Shortly after coming to CDS, John Stearns began to promote the idea of a marketing information system. At every opportunity he would bend Gene Washington's ear and describe how such a system, called the MKIS, could be used not only in marketing research, but also in providing marketing managers with much valuable information. Stearns made the same pitch to other marketing managers who worked out of the Quebec headquarters--Ancel Cluff and the three product managers. Finally, enough of John's enthusiasm rubbed off on the other managers for Gene to agree to a presentation by John to the headquarters staff. Gene thought it would be a good idea to keep IS informed of what was going on, so he issued an invitation to Alton Fox.

On the scheduled date, the headquarters marketing managers and Fox assembled and listened to John Stearns' plan. First, John projected a slide on the screen that listed the three main MKIS objectives.

* Serve as a central repository and distribution center for information from around the world
* Allow quick access to information for marketing and other functional areas
* Provide a flexible network for sharing information among CDS offices worldwide

John went on to explain that the MKIS would provide on-line access to such commercially available databases as Dialog, NewsNet, ICC International Business Research, and Reuters. In addition, the system would have the capability of retrieving data from databases stored on CD-ROM, such as Dun & Bradstreet's Million Dollar and Middle Market Disks, Business America from ABI, and ProPhone.

The combination of this environmental data and internal data from the CDS corporate database would enable marketing research to:

* Identify customer needs for products and services
* Determine the profit potential for particular target markets
* Stay current on the activities of CDS competitors

In addition, the system would serve as a repository of current data and information that marketing managers could draw upon to:

* Stay current on the status of each CDS customer in terms of installed and on-order equipment
* Stay current on potential suppliers of electronic components for CDS products
* Monitor the performance of the CDS sales force

Fox made the point that the regional sales managers would be especially interested in the information relating to customers, products, and sales representatives, and that the product managers could make good use of the information on suppliers. After Stearns had finished, everyone agreed that the idea sounded good.

Sensing an audience just waiting to approve something, Stearns argued for in-house development within marketing, bypassing the formality of getting the project approved by the MIS steering committee. During the short time that Stearns had been on board, he had done his homework and become familiar with the corporate systems development policy. He maintained that the MKIS was more of a decision support system than a management information system and, therefore, could be developed as an end-user application. He also pointed out that the system would be developed within a Windows environment and would feature a graphical user interface. In fact, some of the outputs could incorporate multimedia. Also, the system would be developed using Microsoft Access, a multifeatured database management system that runs on microcomputers and is interfaced with the mainframe database management system. All of these features in a system that was intended to achieve a competitive advantage were exactly what the executive committee was looking for.

Stearns's arguments were strong and there was no question about his computer knowledge and capabilities. So Fox decided that it would be OK for John to do the development within marketing. Gene Washington was happy to get Fox's support and agreed that John could be assisted by his market research analysts, Phyllis Cateora and Bill McCarthey, both of whom were expert in business intelligence databases and Access. Stearns assured Fox and Washington that the system could be developed quickly and would satisfy all of the CDS design standards. Both Washington and Fox gave their blessings, the meeting broke up, and the development project was underway.

For the next several months, Stearns, Cateora, and McCarthey worked away and gradually put the system pieces together. They designed the screens, subscribed to the commercial databases, and obtained the CD-ROMs. They also coordinated with IS to gain access to contents of the accounting information system database relating to customers, products, suppliers, and sales representatives. Contrasted to the external databases, which were generally very current, the AIS data was largely historical.

When the MKIS team had everything in place, Stearns arranged for a demonstration to the same group that had met initially to approve the project. At the demonstration, Cateora did the keyboarding while Stearns explained the system. The MKIS was designed to operate on a microcomputer platform. The micro could download data from the mainframe and store it on its hard drive. Cateora simulated how a manager could use the mouse to specify the information to be displayed, and brought up a series of colorful, dramatic screens. The screens rivaled anything that Steven Spielberg could come up with, combining both graphics and tabular data, and often incorporating audio and video. The screens did an excellent job of providing information to marketing managers on those entities with which the managers would have the greatest interest--customers, suppliers, products, competitors, and marketing representatives.

The Aftermath

Since Stearns was a marketer at heart, he heavily promoted the MKIS to the computer products marketing managers--the regional managers scattered around the world and the managers in the Quebec headquarters, including Washington. Cateora and McCarthey produced an attractive, easy-to-read user manual that explained the steps to follow in retrieving each display. When Washington brought the regional mangers to Quebec for the annual sales planning conference in October of 1999, Cateora conducted hands-on training sessions with the managers, showing each how the system worked.

In addition to promoting the use of the system, Stearns also followed up to ensure that the product met the managers' needs. In December of 1999, he developed a questionnaire that he asked each manager to fill out, describing their satisfaction with the system. The questionnaire appears in Figure 3.

When all of the questionnaires had been returned, Stearns tallied up the responses. Of the nine managers (Washington, the five regional managers, and three product managers), only three indicated that the MKIS contains the types of information they need. Two regional managers explained that they need information about the CDS distribution channel to its customers, including such organizations as mail-order houses and retail stores. Washington noted a need to project activity into the future, such as the effect of changing the commission plan for the sales representatives. One product manager indicated a preference for mathematical models that permit the "trying out" of such decisions as the selection of a particular supplier.

The respondents answered Question 2 by showing some preference for all five categories of information, but with no single category coming close to stimulating universal interest. Washington and the three product managers retrieve product information, three regional managers retrieve customer information, and the product managers all retrieve supplier information. Only one regional manager retrieves information on marketing representatives, and only Washington and a regional manager retrieve information on competitors.

MKIS QUESTIONNAIRE

Name:_____

1. Does the MKIS contain the types of information that you need?
   ___ Yes
   ___ No
   ___ Not sure (Explain:_____)
2. What type(s) of information do you retrieve from the system? (Check all that apply)
   ___ Customer
   ___ Supplier
   ___ Competitor
   ___ Product
   ___ Marketing representative
3. How easy is the system to use?
   ___ Very easy
   ___ Easy
   ___ Difficult
   ___ Very difficult
4. Based on your experience in using the system, how accurate is the information that the MKIS provides?
   ___ Very accurate
   ___ Mostly accurate, but contains a few errors
   ___ Somewhat inaccurate, with more errors than I would like
   ___ Very inaccurate
5. How current is the information that you retrieve?
   ___ Very current
   ___ Mostly current, but contains some outdated information
   ___ Somewhat outdated, with more old data than I would like
   ___ Very outdated information
6. How often do you use the system?
   ___ Several times a day
   ___ About once a day
   ___ Two or three times a week
   ___ Less than two or three times a week
7. How well do you like the MKIS?
   ___ Love it
   ___ Like it
   ___ It's O.K.
   ___ Sort of lukewarm toward it
   ___ Don't really care for it
8. Explain why you feel this way.

   _____

9. How can the system be improved?

   _____

Figure 3

The MKIS User Satisfaction Questionnaire

The system got high marks in terms of accuracy and currency. The response to Question 3 concerning ease of use was positive. All nine managers regarded the MKIS as either "Very easy" or "Easy" to use.

In spite of being easy to use and accurate, the system didn't fare too well in Question 6 as the managers reported a rather low level of use. The three product managers use it several times a day, and Washington about once a day. But, three regional managers reported a use rate of only two or three times a week, and the other two indicated an even less frequency.

The product managers indicated that they "Love" the system, Ancel Cluff and Washington "Like" it, and the other four regional mangers said it's "O.K." In explaining their likes and dislikes, the general feeling of the regional managers was that the system doesn't really meet their needs. The regional managers said that they don't need the system to keep up with the sales representatives since their periodic reports and daily personal contact or e-mail give them everything they need. Washington also stated a satisfaction with the periodic reports he was already receiving and a desire to do more modeling. Surprisingly, neither the regional managers nor the product managers showed any interest in competitive information. The product managers are not too interested in competition, and the regional managers said that they already know all about their competitors, going toe-to-toe with them in the field every day. Although the product managers were very supportive overall, they identified a need for more supplier data from the corporate database, showing the details of how the suppliers' components have performed in the field.

Armed with this information, Stearns talked with each of the out-of-town regional managers by phone, and personally interviewed Cluff and the product managers. The managers' explanations confirmed the survey results. The MKIS wasn't enjoying the high level of use that had been envisioned. Stearns then met with Washington, who acted surprised that the usage was so low.

"I don't use it much myself," Washington explained, "but I'm not a big computer user anyway. I've noticed that the product managers use it a lot and I just assumed that the regional managers liked it too. I'm disappointed that it's not being used. The system wasn't cheap, you know. We spent a lot of money on those commercial databases and CD-ROMs, not to mention the time that you and Phyllis and Bill spent on the coding. You could have been working on something else. Heaven knows, we've got enough marketing research to do. Let me talk with Fox. He's the computer expert and maybe he has an explanation and some advice. Since this is the first time we've tried to develop a system on our own, I really don't know what to tell you."

Later that day, Washington met with Fox, explaining the survey. Fox didn't show any outward signs of emotion, just listening and nodding as Washington laid out the facts.

After Washington had told the whole story, Fox wheeled his chair back from his desk, swiveled around, and began to look through the bottom shelf of his bookcase. "I've got one of my old MIS textbooks here someplace, I think. I might have thrown it away. No, I can't seem to find it." He swiveled back to his desk. "I recall seeing a model of a marketing information system that consisted of input subsystems and output subsystems. When John made his first presentation, I picked up on the fact that his design was all input subsystems. He was entirely concerned with gathering data and putting it in the database. He had no specific details on the output other than some generic screen layouts. After the meeting I asked him about that and he explained that he was taking an enterprise modeling approach by making available all of the data that a marketing manager might ever need. Now, there's nothing wrong with that concept, but you usually have some specific information needs in mind. I think that was John's downfall. When IS does a systems study we spend a lot of time with the user. You know that. We've designed a lot of your reporting systems for you. John assumed too much. He assumed he knew what the managers wanted. In some ways he guessed right. In some ways he guessed wrong. They say experience is the best teacher. I'm sure he'll do better next time."

"Well, Alton, that's not exactly what I wanted to hear. I really need some advice on what we should do now."

Fox got up from his chair and motioned Washington to the door. "Let me call a meeting with my staff and we'll see if we can generate some ideas. I'll get back to you as soon as I have something. Don't worry. It's spilt milk. We have a lot of options. Always do. That's one of the good things about this business."

QUESTIONS:

1. In what way or ways has CDS done a good job of establishing a policy of information resources management? In what way or ways has CDS not done a good job?

2. Does CDS set a good example for its customers in terms of how it uses its own products? Support your answer.

3. What are the advantages, if any, of the CDS policy that requires organizational systems to be implemented in a top-down fashion, and individual user or work group systems to be implemented bottom-up? What are the disadvantages?

4. Assuming that there is a problem at CDS, what is it and where does it exist within the organization?

5. Was Stearns right in maintaining that the MKIS was more of a DSS than an MIS? Explain.

6. Identify each person who contributed to the development of a system that did not achieve its expected use. List their names, describe the error(s) of each, and rank them from the most responsible to least responsible for the overall results.

7. Now, for each person named in question 6, specify the action that each should have taken.

8. Recognizing that this same situation could happen again and again, what would you do to prevent a recurrence? Be specific in terms of the organizational level where your solution would be aimed and what action you would recommend.

9. Alton Fox agreed to let John Stearns do the development of the MKIS within the marketing group as an end-user application. Should Fox have argued that Stearn's proposal was likely to fail? Should Fox have suggested the proposal be reviewed by the MIS steering committee?

McLeod / Schell Case Solution Form 1
The Problem Setting

Case: <u>Canadian Data Systems, Ltd.</u>　　　　**Name:** _____

Environmental Elements:

Important Facts:

McLeod / Schell Case Solution Form 2
Elements of the Firm as a System

Case: **Canadian Data Systems, Ltd.**　　　　Name: _____

Objectives and/or Standards:

Output:

Management and Organization:

Information Processor:

Inputs and Input Resources:

Transformation Process:

Output Resources:

McLeod / Schell Case Solution Form 3
Subsystems of the Firm

Case: <u>**Canadian Data Systems, Ltd.**</u>   **Name:** _____

Subsystem:

Subsystem:

Subsystem:

Subsystem:

McLeod / Schell Case Solution Form 4
Problems and Symptoms

Case: <u>Canadian Data Systems, Ltd.</u>　　　　Name: _____

Environment:
Objectives and/or Standards:
Output:
Management and Organization:
Information Processor:
Inputs and Physical System:

Main Problem(s):

1.

2.

3.

McLeod / Schell Case Solution Form 5
Alternatives

Case: <u>Canadian Data Systems, Ltd.</u> **Name:** _____

Alternative:

  Advantages:

  Disadvantages:

Alternative:

  Advantages:

  Disadvantages:

McLeod / Schell Case Solution Form 5
Alternatives

Case: **Canadian Data Systems, Ltd.**　　　　　Name: _____

Alternative:

　Advantages:

　Disadvantages:

Alternative:

　Advantages:

　Disadvantages:

McLeod / Schell Case Solution Form 6
Decision and Implementation

Case: **Canadian Data Systems, Ltd.**　　　　　Name: _____

Decision:

Implementation Resources Needed:

Implementation Steps to be Followed:

BALTIMORE DOOR & WINDOW

Baltimore Door & Window (BDW) is a company headquartered in Baltimore, Maryland that manufactures and sells a line of building and home repair products consisting primarily of doors, windows, and skylights. Although the scale of operation has grown exponentially since the company was founded in 1922, all of the production is performed at the manufacturing complex in Baltimore. Shipments are made to distribution centers in Europe, South America, and Africa, as well as the U.S. and Canada.

The first BDW product was a wooden door with a stained-glass window and intricate carving, designed for use as the front door of luxury homes. Over the years the product line was broadened to include other types of doors and windows and, most recently, skylights. The current product line consists of over 250 separate products, many coming in a variety of colors and sizes. The original strategy of emphasizing quality proved sound, and today BDW is one of the leading manufacturers in the world of building and home repair products.

A Customer Orientation

In addition to the emphasis on quality, BDW's success can also be attributed to an awareness of the environment in which it operates. BDW executives have always favored a proactive, rather than reactive, posture in relation to its environmental elements, especially its customers, competitors, suppliers, and the government.

The marketing division has responsibility for keeping BDW in contact with its customers, monitoring satisfaction with current products and anticipating future needs. Some of this information is gathered by the BDW marketing representatives as they cover their territories, but most is gathered by the marketing research department. The marketing research department monitors the economy, analyzes government statistics, and conducts a variety of surveys.

A good example of how its environmental focus has paid off was the recognition by marketing research in the early 1980s that high energy costs would force homeowners to remodel their homes to make them more fuel efficient. Marketing research foresaw that the homeowners would install insulation in the attic and would replace old-fashioned doors and windows with double-pane units that greatly reduce heat transfer.

Rather than wait for the market to demand more energy efficient doors and windows, BDW changed its production facilities and purchased the automated machine tools necessary to handle these new products before its competitors could act. BDW purchased the equipment when it was new on the market and demand was relatively low. This perfect timing enabled BDW to obtain the equipment at bargain prices. Their competitors, on the other hand, waited until demand increased and were forced to pay high prices for new equipment. BDW's manufacturing costs have always been lower than those of its competitors because of the economies that were realized in the assembly of its production facilities.

Another example of vision and insight on the part of BDW top management is the early identification of do-it-yourself homeowners as a potentially large and profitable market. BDW marketers correctly predicted that many homeowners would prefer to repair their existing homes rather than purchase new ones, and would rather do the work themselves than pay someone else.

Although an orientation to the do-it-yourself market seems like an easy strategy to implement, there was much more to it than an advertising campaign. An integral part of the BDW efforts was a broad-based educational program aimed at teaching homeowners the benefits of doing their own home repairs. The company sponsored a series of programs for educational TV stations that showed how homes can be made more energy efficient. Although a variety of methods were demonstrated, the replacement and installation of windows, doors, and skylights received the most attention. To complement the educational programs, BDW managers regularly spoke to civic clubs and high schools about such topics as the importance of energy conservation, the influence of proper maintenance on real estate value, and how homeowners can obtain low-interest loans for home repair.

Whereas the educational program was the most visible evidence of BDW's new strategy, the real key was the product line. Many of the products were reengineered so that they could be installed with the standard tools that are ordinarily found around the home--hammer, pliers, and screwdriver. In those cases where a special tool was necessary, it was included in the product kit so that the buyer did not have to make a special trip to the store. Nails, screws, bolts, and other hardware were also included in the kit. Instructions in the product kits were written in everyday language, using no technical terms, and color illustrations were provided for each step of the installation process to match the color coding on the product being installed. Hundreds of field tests were conducted around the world to ensure that average homeowners could understand and follow the do-it-yourself instructions.

When a homeowner purchased a BDW product and successfully installed it, he or she became "sold" on the company and passed the word along to friends, neighbors, coworkers, and relatives. This word-of-mouth advertising supplemented the radio, TV, newspaper, and magazine ads that promoted the use of BDW products and the economics of do-it-yourself home improvement.

The strategy of aiming at the home improvement market was a big departure for BDW. The original profile of the BDW customer, on whom the company's original success had been built, was an affluent husband and wife team purchasing several high-priced items for an expensive new home. In most cases a single sale would exceed $5,000. Conversely, the current customer can be a young married couple or single parent usually purchasing only one item at a relatively low price. The number of customers in the do-it-yourself market is much larger, however, producing sales revenues today that far exceed the wildest dreams of the company founders.

Today's BDW executives, supported by marketing research data, anticipate that the annual sales growth will continue for the foreseeable future. In order to make that growth pay off, it will be necessary to keep costs low to realize the largest profit possible.

Innovation in Products and Services

Other examples of innovative ideas can be found in practically all areas of BDW operations. One is the toll-free customer hotline, which was installed to answer customer questions and hear the few customer complaints. The hotline operates around the clock, seven days a week, and is staffed by multilingual personnel especially trained to handle calls in a friendly, knowledgeable way.

Probably the most innovative idea came as the result of the company's employee suggestion program. An employee in the shipping department, who had purchased and installed some BDW products, suggested that the packing materials be designed so that they could aid in product installation. For example, the spacers that cushion windows in the crate could be used during installation to properly align and plumb the window in its frame. This idea was incorporated into the packing of all products and, in effect, enabled BDW to provide installation aids to their customers at no extra cost.

An Emphasis on Employee Education

A less obvious reason for BDW's success is its comprehensive employee education program. Originally implemented in the years following the Great Depression of the early 1930s, the program is designed to provide BDW employees with the knowledge and skills required to do their jobs. Employees on all levels attend classes and seminars sponsored by the human resources division, trade associations, and colleges and universities that enable the employees to remain up-to-date on the latest technologies and methodologies.

During recent years, these educational programs have included an increasing number of courses designed to make employees computer literate. The company offers a complete set of courses in both hardware and software used at BDW. The hardware courses cover such units as keyboard terminals and microcomputers, and the software courses deal with word processing, electronic spreadsheets, graphics packages, database query languages, desktop publishing, and project management systems. Special versions of these courses are tailored especially to managers and provide examples of management applications. All of the courses are taught by personnel from the BDW information services (IS) division.

Pioneer Computing Applications at BDW

The company was one of the first users of computers for data processing. BDW opened its data center in the late 1950s with the installation of a medium-size computer, an IBM 650. The first applications included the bread-and-butter accounting applications--payroll, order entry, inventory, billing, accounts receivable, and general ledger. As soon as the bugs settled out, top-level management decided to expand into the manufacturing area. The first step was the installation of a data collection system as a way of gathering data in real time as production processes occurred. Data collection terminals were located throughout the shop floor and inventory areas and used for attendance and job reporting. As the BDW workers performed their tasks they entered data into the terminals by means of the keyboard, punched cards, and the badge reader. This data gathering system, one of the first in the country, enabled the IBM 650 to provide manufacturing management with a current picture of the production operation. The BDW managers learned about problems and opportunities while there was still time to act, whereas their competitors, with less responsive systems, could only sit on the sidelines and watch.

When the data collection application began to take most of the available computer time, the IBM 650 was replaced with a larger mainframe. The data processing applications were expanded to include manufacturing control, which involved "exploding" the bills of material to identify the gross raw materials inventory required to produce the finished products. These gross requirements were compared to the raw materials on hand to determine which items had to be reordered--the net requirements. Use of the computer in this manner to determine inventory replenishment needs led to the addition of follow-on data processing applications--purchasing, receiving, and accounts payable.

By 1965 BDW had computerized all of its data processing applications in the accounting and manufacturing areas and had another new mainframe computer with high capacity disk storage units and remote terminals located throughout the Baltimore headquarters and plant facilities. The terminals enabled all of the users to run their jobs on the powerful mainframe, an application called time-sharing. During this period, networked systems were rare and firms such as BDW were viewed as innovators.

BDW continued its leadership in manufacturing computing during the 1970s by implementing a material requirements planning (MRP) system, which reflected a proactive view towards production. Rather than wait for raw material inventory items to reach their reorder points to trigger the purchase of replenishment stock, BDW manufacturing management projected the production schedule for as far as a year or more into the future to determine their inventory needs. This approach was named materials requirements planning (MRP), and was later expanded to include the other major BDW organizational units--marketing and finance. Such an expanded system is named MRP-II, manufacturing resource planning. More recently, the computer-based manufacturing applications have incorporated just-in-time manufacturing, which demands intricate coordination with suppliers, and computer-integrated manufacturing (CIM), which makes heavy use of robotics.

Information-Oriented Computer Applications

The solid integration of computer applications in manufacturing is reflective of computer use throughout BDW. Every functional area and department has incorporated the computer into its processing, with the evolution following the same pattern that occurred in manufacturing. Computer resources were first used for data processing and then focused on decision support. By the mid-1980s, BDW had successfully expanded their data processing system to include a management information system, hundreds of decision support systems, and both organizational and individual office automation applications.

The Management Information System. The BDW MIS consists primarily of a marketing information system (MKIS) and a human resource information system (HRIS). A few years ago several senior managers expressed interest in an executive information system but IS had its hands full with other projects and could not make the necessary staff available. After a few months of inaction, the senior managers lost interest.

The experiences in marketing of applying the MIS concept have been much more productive. The MKIS was originally installed around 1970 and consists mainly of periodic reports and mathematical models. Marketing managers use the models to assign sales representatives to territories, set prices for the firm's products, and determine routes to use in delivering products through the complex BDW distribution channel. Much of marketing database that provides inputs to the reports and models consists of primary data gathered by the marketing research department. Other data comes in the form of commercial business intelligence databases to which BDW subscribes.

The human resource information system currently being developed is the most recent example of an MIS oriented to the needs of a functional area. The project has been a cooperative effort involving information specialists from both the human resources (HR) and IS divisions. HR originally wanted to assemble its own staff of information specialists but had difficulty because of some internal management problems. As a result, IS has had to do most of the development work and has not been able to staff the project at the necessary level.

When the HRIS is eventually implemented it will become the complete responsibility of HR. The plan is for HR to maintain all of the software developed by IS for the original system as well as develop new systems. However, HR's ability to build up its staff of information specialists to the necessary level is still in question.

Decision Support Systems. Most of the decision support systems (DSSs) exist in the form of electronic spreadsheets and databases on PCs. These systems were developed by users in a controlled environment, as mandated by company policy. End-users were required to justify their applications and obtain approval for acquisition of the necessary resources. IS personnel worked closely with the end-users and provided training. IS also provided guidelines to ensure that the end-user applications did not contaminate the corporate database and compromise computer security. This "hand holding" by IS has paid off in the form of a diverse portfolio of end-user applications but it has not been without its price. The long hours spent with end-users meant that IS could not find time to develop many organizational systems. As a result, there is an estimated two-year backlog of applications waiting for IS to develop for users and run in the data center.

Office Automation. BDW got involved in office automation (OA) like most other companies, in a piecemeal fashion with no grand plan. First, it was word processing, followed by electronic mail. E-mail was implemented top-down, beginning in the executive suite. The executives quickly became enthusiastic e-mail supporters and the lower-level managers took the hint and began clamoring to get on the network. Today e-mail and voice mail serve as communications media for BDW personnel on all levels, in all parts of the world. Other OA applications that have been implemented on a firm-wide basis include electronic calendaring, audio and video conferencing, and document imaging. All of these systems were developed in accordance with corporate guidelines.

Additional OA applications have been implemented on a local basis to meet needs of individuals and small work groups. These applications, including word processing, FAX, and desktop publishing, have generally been implemented free from corporate constraint. Users must only receive approval from their immediate superior and a PC committee, which reviews all requests. Approval is usually automatic.

Expert Systems. Despite efforts to integrate artificial intelligence in the company operations, accomplishments thus far have been modest. A group of finance professors from a local university developed an expert system to analyze monthly financial reports submitted by BDW subsidiaries. The system makes value judgments concerning the stability of the subsidiaries and is able to detect possible fraud. A $100,000 scam in a foreign operation that had evaded the human financial analysts for months was detected by the expert system the first time it was used.

The manufacturing area also uses an expert system for assembly line balancing. As the work flows down the assembly line, inputs from electronic sensors and the data collection network identify problems that might be caused by the work flowing faster or slower than scheduled. The expert system notifies the shop floor supervisors so that they can take corrective action. This system was a joint effort combining the production expertise of BDW industrial engineers and the knowledge acquisition ability of an expert system software consulting firm. IS played only a minor role in development.

The application of expert systems in marketing has been the most difficult due to the unstructured nature of many of the problems. Several efforts to implement systems have failed, but one is still in the process of being validated. It is an expert system that monitors the levels of BDW products in retailers' stores and automatically replenishes the stock when necessary, eliminating the need for the retailers to prepare purchase orders. Systems analysts from IS have had difficulty in capturing the logic that the retailers follow because of the wide variance in practices. If these problems are not worked out in the next few months, the project will be scrapped.

All of these examples show that BDW management has strived to apply the computer to its operations in a most thorough way. The large number of applications, the manner in which they span both data processing and decision support, and their presence in all functional areas are evidence of the commitment by top management to get maximum mileage from its information resources.

Current BDW Information Resources

The BDW information resources consist of hardware, information specialists, software and data. An IBM mainframe located in the IS data center is presently being used as the host computer in the BDW computer network, which includes both distributed processors and terminals. Minicomputers systems similar to the one in human resources are also located in finance and marketing. The number of data collection terminals in the production area has grown to almost 300 and there are approximately one thousand keydriven terminals and microcomputers located in user offices. The 14 distribution centers are connected to headquarters with leased communications lines and also have small business computers equipped with high-speed printers used to prepare large-volume printouts.

Information Specialists. The hardware and software is supported by a staff of approximately 375 information specialists, with almost 300 located in the IS department. The remainder are in user areas.

Most of the analysts, programmers, and database administrators in IS are assigned to new systems development projects, but the maintenance of existing systems is exerting more and more of a resource drain. In 1990 about 25 percent of these specialists' time was spent on maintenance but the figure had grown to 35 percent in 1995 and 47 percent by the summer of 2000. IS management expects the percentage to increase by about 3 percent per year and eventually level off at about 75 percent. The managers base their projections on what has happened in other companies similar to BDW. If this continued increase in the maintenance workload takes place it will mean that new systems development will be seriously curtailed. Only those systems that have the highest priority will be implemented.

On the plus side, there is a high degree of professionalism among the information specialists. Eighty-five percent have college degrees, with most of the majors being in MIS or computer science. Some of the specialists have graduate degrees and some are active in professional organizations. Although the salary scale at BDW is no higher than other large companies in the area, there is a good benefits program, resulting in a minimum of employee turnover. Only about 5 percent of the information specialists leave each year, usually to accept managerial jobs with other firms.

Software Resources. In terms of its software resources, BDW has over 200 organizational systems in full operation. Most are large systems consisting of multiple computer programs. There are approximately 15 COBOL legacy programs, most of which were developed in-house during the 1970s. Some of the organizational systems have been in use for twenty years or more, but most have been developed within the last five years. Some computer programs were designed prior to structured programming techniques and exist in the form of "spaghetti code." Most of the documentation is good, but in some cases it consists of only source program listings.

Data Resources. The BDW corporate database is managed by IBM's DB2 database management system and supports the data processing, MIS, and many of the decision support and expert system applications. Most of this data is provided by the data processing system, but some is obtained from vendors of commercial databases. Most of the end-user decision support systems use microcomputer-based database management systems, such as Access. Since BDW has encouraged computer use for so long most of the corporate data is in a computer form. Very seldom is a user faced with an application that requires data not already in the computer.

Strategic Planning at BDW

Twenty years ago, BDW president Harold Butler realized that the company needed a more formal method of planning at the corporate level, and engaged the assistance of the Zymurgy Group. A one-week meeting with the Zymurgy Group was held in Hamilton, N.Y., attended by the president and all division vice presidents. This meeting laid the foundation for a consistent corporate planning methodology. At the heart of BDW strategic planning are the annual and monthly meetings of the corporate planning committee (CPC).

The Corporate Planning Committee. The CPC consists of the group of BDW executives who are responsible for corporate strategy. In many firms this group is called the executive committee. The CPC includes Butler as the chair, vice president of finance Joan McLane, vice president of manufacturing Milton Winfield, vice president of marketing Gene Posey, and vice president of administration, John Moseley.

Each year a CPC meeting is held away from the Baltimore headquarters for the purpose of specifying the corporate strategic activity for the coming planning period. A trained planning coordinator plans the agenda and conducts the sessions, which span a two-and-a-half-day period.

The annual meeting concludes with a decision concerning the critical issues for the coming year. The critical issues change little from year to year but are influenced by the degree to which BDW can achieve improvements in automation, and recruit and retain quality employees to meet the sales, production, and support objectives.

In addition to the annual meeting, the CPC meets each month to discuss progress toward the plan, re-evaluate the plan in light of social and business changes, and make modifications when necessary.

The Strategic Business Plan. The first strategic business plans were bottom-up efforts based on information from lower-level managers that defined market opportunities. As BDW operations became more widespread, top management recognized the need for greater focus on long-term objectives and the bottom-up approach gave way to the top-down approach that is currently being followed.

The strategic business plan does not explicitly describe computer applications. Rather, it states as corporate policy that the primary objective of the firm's information systems is to achieve competitive advantage and encourage end-user computing. It also states a dedication to ethical computer use and the protection of individuals' right to privacy. The accomplishment of these objectives is left to the MIS planning committee.

The MIS Planning Committee

The MIS planning committee has more authority than is normally associated with MIS steering committees. Whereas steering committees usually have the responsibility for achieving strategic plans that someone else has made, the MIS planning committee has the responsibility for making those plans as well as carrying them out.

All of the members of the CPC except Butler are also members of the MIS planning committee. Additional members of the MIS committee include the vice president of information services Melinda Morris, and the vice president of human resources, Helen Douglass. In the BDW organizational structure, Morris and Douglass both report to the vice president of administration, Moseley. The other vice presidents report to Butler.

The MIS planning committee convenes for a lengthy session each year when it develops the strategic plan for information systems, and meets weekly during the rest of the year when it monitors systems projects. The weekly meetings consist of discussions of the weekly written reports submitted by the project team leaders, plus occasional oral reports from the team leaders or members, or other specialists who have some particular expertise that bears on the problems at hand.

The Strategic Plan for Information Systems

The strategic plan for information systems projects computer use for the coming three years. It addresses each basic type of information resource (personnel, hardware, software, and data) for each of the major application areas--data processing, MIS, DSS, office automation, and expert systems. It also includes an end-user computing strategy.

As in most companies, the BDW information resources were originally concentrated in the data center. The rise of end-user computing prompted the MIS planning committee to respond in the mid-1980s by creating an information center (IC). The IC is a special facility in the main headquarters building that contains both hardware and software that end-users can use to do their own work.

For several years end-user computing was concentrated in the IC. Then, around 1990 when it became evident that end-users were going to insist on having their own equipment, the MIS planning committee established the PC committee, not as a way to suppress PC purchases but to ensure that they conform to certain guidelines. The policy worked well and has resulted in a reduced utilization of the IC. Now, the IC is open only during normal working hours and the help desk is staffed by the IC manager, Caroline Mitchell. The IC is a part of IS, and Mitchell reports to Melinda Morris.

The Chief Information Officer

Melinda Morris was hired as vice president of information services three years ago and functions as the chief information officer (CIO). When she applied for the job, the BDW executives were impressed with her solid business background. She has a masters degree in information systems and rose through the ranks of an information systems consulting firm, first as an analyst and then as a management consultant. This experience put her in good stead with those executives who have strong managerial leanings and is one of the reasons why she is treated with more respect than her predecessors, who were regarded as technicians.

The IC Issue

One day Morris was in her office and Caroline Mitchell walked in. The two began to chat and Mitchell expressed her concern over the lack of activity in the IC. "There's really not much for me to do any more. The only real user is marketing research and they don't need my help. I feel like I'm just wasting my time and I'm sure we could find a better use for all the hardware and software."

Morris promised to bring the subject up at the next MIS planning committee meeting, which she did a couple of days later. After explaining the situation the other members began to voice their views.

The only person who opposed shutting down the operation was Gene Posey, the vice president of marketing. Posey maintained that the center was critical to performing the marketing research function and he especially liked the fact that the center was located just across the hall and was never crowded. It was like marketing research had its own private information system consultants.

The issue was quickly resolved when a decision was reached to move some of the resources to marketing research and relocate the remainder to other user areas. But the IC discussion somehow put the members in a reflective mood and they began to question the way that BDW meets all of its information needs. During the next hour or so the various members made suggestions that could dramatically alter how BDW performed its information processing.

The first suggestion was offered by Milton Winfield, the vice president of manufacturing, who recommended a greater reliance on prewritten software. "We've had extremely good luck with the MRP-II systems. Melinda, not to be critical of the IS staff, but the quality of prewritten software is much higher than we would be able to achieve if your people had done the work. IS just doesn't understand manufacturing as well as the programmers that wrote the packages. I think we should stop being so provincial about systems development and give the 'buy' a lot more consideration when we make the 'make or buy' decision."

Joan McLane, the vice president of finance picked up on Winfield's suggestion. "We could do the same thing in accounting. There are so many prewritten data processing systems these days. We can find payroll, inventory, receivables, and payables packages that do exactly what we want done, at a fraction of what we would spend developing them ourselves. Melinda, I think IS could get out of the system development business altogether and we would never miss a beat."

These suggestions were kicked around for a while and nobody seriously objected, including Morris. Her only concern was that the corporate database be protected, pointing out that most of its contents were provided by data processing applications. Morris was extremely open-minded about computer use and would never protect her own turf if it was clear that work should be done somewhere else. The general agreement was that when future systems development projects come up, a special effort should be made to determine whether prewritten software exists.

Just as it appeared that the meeting was winding down, John Moseley, the vice president of administration, offered an even more dramatic suggestion.

John Mosley: One alternative that we have never seriously considered is outsourcing. Melinda, I know that you outsource the hardware maintenance, but everybody does that. We could never justify having our own staff of field engineers. But I'm talking about outsourcing everything, and I mean everything. We all know about the Kodak decision to outsource and it seems like everyone is jumping on the bandwagon. Are we missing something by not giving it more attention?

Gene Posey: You're right about the bandwagon. I read that the Yankee Group consulting firm estimated that 20 percent of the Fortune 500 firms were outsourcing by 1994. Now with all of the enterprise resource planning systems put in by SAP, Oracle, and the other vendors, it seems as if outsourcing is the only possible outcome for the future. We've always regarded IS as a way to maintain an edge on our competition. But American Airlines, who wrote the book on information systems for competitive advantage with the SABRE system for airline reservations, regards computing as a commodity. Didn't their head of the SABRE system joke that having a vice president of information systems is like having a vice president of electricity or gas?

Melinda Morris: Well, that's certainly a career path I can follow if you people do away with IS. And you know the Kodak story was an initial success, but three years after outsourcing they discovered major problems with the arrangement. A lot of the outsourced systems were brought back inside Kodak.

Gene Posey: (quick to console Melinda) You don't have anything to worry about, Melinda. I know that IS has problems keeping up with demand but it's because you've done such a good job. You've got so many successful systems running that your people spend a lot of time maintaining them instead of designing new systems. And users are anxious to do their own computing but can't do it without a lot of help from you. So, don't worry about looking for another title. We couldn't get along without you or IS.

Joan McLane: I've heard that some companies are saving 20 to 50 percent on their computer expenses. If there's that kind of potential, we should be considering it.

Melinda Morris: I'm not saying that we shouldn't consider outsourcing, but there is more to it than meets the eye. The companies that save the most are companies that had poorly run information systems functions. Sure, some companies have been able to save a bundle, but others have tried it and gotten burned. That's where the term "insourcing" came from. But bringing back a computer application is not so easy once you've let it go. You could end up with no capability for doing your own work and it would take years to recover. There's a definite down side to outsourcing and if we decide to pursue it, then we must examine it from all angles.

John Moseley: Melinda, I'm sure you know more about it than any of us. What are some of the risks?

Melinda Morris: Well, for starters, you're putting a very important business function into the hands of outsiders. They don't know BDW like our own IS staff knows us. If the outsourcers go out of business or don't perform as expected, we could really suffer. BDW uses information systems for critical systems and operations. Another big consideration is our employees. What would happen if we decide to outsource a big portion of our operation, as Kodak did? How would that affect our computer people? Most firms that outsource a large portion of their operations see many key IS employees move to other companies.

Gene Posey: Very often the employees go to work for the outsourcer don't they?

Melinda Morris: Initially that's true, but sometimes the outsourcing firm lays off those employees within a year of the outsource date. There have been stories of how some outsourcers pick up a staff to finish the projects that are under development and then let the staff go when the work is done. Our employees would see the change as a definite loss of job security. The human resources consideration is very important.

John Moseley: Melinda, are there any real benefits that we could expect, outside the chance to cut some of our costs?

Melinda Morris: By outsourcing some of our legacy systems--the electricity and gas that Gene mentioned--we could pay more attention to those applications that have a strategic value, such as the executive information system that we shelved a while back. That could be a real advantage, allowing us to concentrate our resources on developing new information systems where our IS people would do the most good.
   There's no doubt we're going to have to get some relief. We can't go on like we are now. With the build-up of systems maintenance and end-user computing our staff just won't be able to keep up. But, we shouldn't just look at the low end of the scale. Another argument in favor of outsourcing is that it enables you to quickly acquire expertise that you don't have in-house. We've got an excellent staff, probably one of the best in the country, but we could use some help in certain areas. Manufacturing resource planning software is an area where we need more expertise. What I'm saying is that there are certain application areas where outsourcing could be a real benefit.

John Moseley: Maybe it's not an all or nothing sort of thing. We could outsource only certain applications. But I would like for us to go into it open-minded. The same goes for prewritten software. I think we should consider outsourcing or prewritten software for everything and see where that path leads us.

Melinda Morris: (nodding in agreement) I can't believe that the IC problem started all this but I'm glad it came up. It's long overdue. We need to give this a thorough review.

John Moseley: Let's all think about it and when we meet next week maybe someone will have some good ideas. Meeting adjourned.

QUESTIONS:

1. Rate overall computer use at BDW. How would you classify it: Excellent, Good, Average, or Poor? Support your rating with a paragraph or two using examples from the case.

2. Choose a problem in terms of how BDW is using its information resources. What is it? Whose responsibility is it? How did arise?

3. Should BDW consider greater use of prewritten software? For what reasons? Which applications are the best candidates? Be specific.

4. Make a list of at least three benefits that are possible through outsourcing. Don't limit yourself to the ones that were discussed in the meeting. Supplement the case material with other sources--your text and articles. For each benefit indicate how much potential it holds for BDW. Use the descriptors "Much potential," "Little potential," and "Unknown."

5. Make a similar list, with descriptors, for the possible risks associated with outsourcing.

6. Assume that BDW will have to decide whether to pursue custom programming, use of prewritten software, or outsourcing for each of its applications, what would you recommend? Consider groups of applications such as accounting, materials resource planning, and end-user computing. Support your recommendations.

McLeod / Schell Case Solution Form 1
The Problem Setting

Case: <u>Baltimore Door & Window</u>   **Name:** _____

Environmental Elements:

Important Facts:

McLeod / Schell Case Solution Form 2
Elements of the Firm as a System

Case: **Baltimore Door & Window**   Name: _____

Objectives and/or Standards:
Output:
Management and Organization:
Information Processor:
Inputs and Input Resources:
Transformation Process:
Output Resources:

McLeod / Schell Case Solution Form 3
Subsystems of the Firm

Case: <u>Baltimore Door & Window</u>   **Name:** _____

Subsystem:

Subsystem:

Subsystem:

Subsystem:

McLeod / Schell Case Solution Form 4
Problems and Symptoms

Case: **Baltimore Door & Window** Name: _____

Environment:
Objectives and/or Standards:
Output:
Management and Organization:
Information Processor:
Inputs and Physical System:

Main Problem(s):

1.

2.

3.

McLeod / Schell Case Solution Form 5
Alternatives

Case: <u>Baltimore Door & Window</u> **Name:** _____

Alternative:

  Advantages:

  Disadvantages:

Alternative:

  Advantages:

  Disadvantages:

McLeod / Schell Case Solution Form 5
Alternatives

Case: Baltimore Door & Window   **Name:** _____

Alternative:

  Advantages:

  Disadvantages:

Alternative:

  Advantages:

  Disadvantages:

McLeod / Schell Case Solution Form 6
Decision and Implementation

Case: <u>**Baltimore Door & Window**</u>   **Name:** _____

Decision:

Implementation Resources Needed:

Implementation Steps to be Followed: